P9-DWE-503

DATE DUE

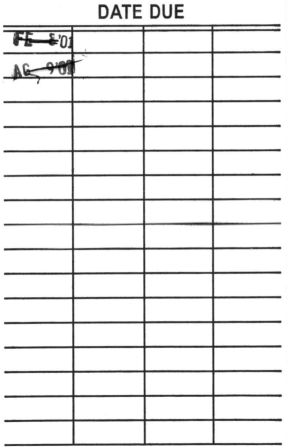

FE 8'01

AG 9'01

THE
REFERENCE
SHELF

FREE TRADE VERSUS

PROTECTIONISM

edited by HENRÍ MILLER

THE REFERENCE SHELF

Volume 68 Number 4

THE H. W. WILSON COMPANY

New York   Dublin   1996

ELF

f articles, excerpts from
social trends in the Unit-
nbers to a volume, all of
dar year. Numbers one
t, give background infor-
mation and discussion from various points of view, concluding with a
comprehensive bibliography that contains books, pamphlets, and abstracts of additional articles on the subject. The final number is a collec-
tion of recent speeches. This number also contains a subject index to the
entire Reference Shelf volume. Books in the series may be purchased indi-
vidually or on subscription.

Visit our web site at: http://www.hwwilson.com

Library of Congress Cataloging-in-Publication Data

Main entry under title:

Free trade versus protectionism / edited by Henri Miller.
    p. cm. — (The Reference shelf ; v. 68, no. 4)
   Includes bibliographical references.
   ISBN 0-8242-0889-7
   1. Free trade.   2. Protectionism.   3. Free trade—North America.
4.General Agreement on Tariffs and Trade (Organization)
I. Miller, Henri.   II. Series.
HF1704.F743   1996
382'.7—dc20

96-8676
CIP

Cover: A crane loads cargo onto a ship. *Photo:* Bettmann

Printed in the United States of America

CONTENTS

PREFACE

The historic debate over free trade versus protectionism continues to plague nations, including the United States. Part of the problem lies with the threat of war; for reasons of national security, countries do not wish to be dependent on foreign supplies. They look within themselves and follow the policy of protectionism by raising prices—through tariffs or special taxes—on foreign goods and by restricting the amount of certain goods that people may bring into the country. In peacetime, however, most countries want to buy and sell freely, without restrictions, but their trading policies conflict with most other countries.

Less-developed nations use tariffs to protect smaller industries, as the United States did in the 1880s. Today, however, the U.S. has shifted toward free trade, except in agriculture. Supporters of free trade argue that protectionism leads to national isolationism, international rivalries, and even threats of war; however, even those countries most in favor of free trade usually see a need for some form of protectionism.

The General Agreement on Tariffs and Trade (GATT), established shortly after World War II, was a major aid to multilateral negotiations. Despite GATT's success, it was only a temporary solution. The latest international meetings called the *Uruguay Round*—finalized in 1994—expanded provisions of GATT, promised lower trade barriers, and slashed tariffs by an average of one-third. These meetings also laid the foundation for future talks dealing with the establishment of the World Trade Organization (WTO) to succeed GATT.

In 1993, U.S. president George Bush proposed the North American Free Trade Agreement (NAFTA), as a set of trading privileges for businesses in the U.S., Mexico, and Canada. With increasing popularity, free trade agreements within regional trade blocs, such as the European Union (EU), NAFTA and the impending Association of Southeast Asian Nations (ASEAN) began to set their own rules of trade, encouraging cooperative exchanges but hinting at protectionism against countries outside the region.

Section One, "Past Mistakes, New Trade Politics, and Beyond," supplies background information on global trade. A speech by Robert P. Forrestal discusses international trading zones, while the next two articles identify the problems and missed opportunities of past trade agreements. Looking toward the future, articles from *New Perspectives Quarterly* and *National Review* assess the potential for global free trade as well as new developments.

One of the latest adjustments to free trade has been the North American Free Trade Agreement. "NAFTA's Results," Section Two, views NAFTA from several different perspectives. The opening article from *Reason* explains the components that make up this new trade agreement. Subsequent articles from *USA Today*, *The New York Times*, and *Audubon* show the negative impact the agreement has had on job competition, drug enforcement, and the environment. With the upcoming 1996 election in mind, "Fair Trade, Foul Politics" presents NAFTA's role in domestic politics. The section ends with a status report from *The Nation* on NAFTA.

"Policy Controversy," Section Three, shows how trade policies have led to controversies over such products as bananas, drugs, and textiles, without, however, managing to save jobs. Articles from *Commonweal*, *New Perspectives Quarterly*, and *Challenge* explain various controversial situations brought on by foreign trade. Articles from *The Nation* and *Ms.* reveal how—in some cases—free trade agreements have actually caused the loss of jobs.

Section Four, "A World of Indecision," completes the compilation by observing various approaches to trade used by different countries. Focusing on the United States, the opening article gives a short history of U.S. trade and explains how the country has expanded because of trade advantages. Articles from *The New York Times* and *Society* explain how other countries are beginning to recognize their changing needs for foreign trade. Finally, *The Economist* examines the trade policies of South Korea, a strongly protectionist nation.

The editor would like to thank the authors and publishers who have granted permission to reprint their material in this compilation.

HENRí MILLER

April 1996

I. PAST MISTAKES, NEW TRADE POLITICS, AND BEYOND

Editor's Introduction

In foreign policy, new decisions constantly alter the provisions within trade agreements. This section reviews the history of those changes and looks to the future for protectionism and free trade. Section One begins with an International Business Lecture delivered by Robert P. Forrestal, reprinted from *Vital Speeches of the Day*. His address analyzes major trading zones of the world: the Americas, Western Europe, and the Asian-Pacific region. The author also summarizes the economic conditions of potential trading partners in Latin America. As an advocate of free trade, Forrestal believes it is imperative for the United States to be "competitive . . . and for each American to understand that for every challenge in that global marketplace, there are many opportunities."

In the second article, Sam A. Pitroda, writing in the *Harvard International Review*, describes some problems with the General Agreement on Tariffs and Trade (GATT) and the potential role of the World Trade Organization (WTO) in addressing those problems. Pitroda feels the WTO will discipline countries in areas of agriculture, food services, and intellectual property, and also clarify dumping regulations, subsidies, quota restrictions, and voluntary export restraints.

"Dutch Tulips and Emerging Markets," the next article, reprinted from *Foreign Affairs*, discusses the expansion of global markets. The author, Paul Krugman, argues that substantial involvement in international trade can only help U.S. businesses. He considers this the central theme of the Clinton administration's economic strategy. However, Krugman warns that another disaster like the Mexican currency crisis could result in an economic downturn at home.

The fourth article, reprinted from *New Perspectives Quarterly*, draws attention to a loss of jobs due to technological innovations and how competition will affect free trade. Paul Kennedy's article, "The Threat of Modernization," questions the benefits of automation that is designed to reduce the workforce. Politicians, reluctant to address issues like immigration and population growth, argue instead about the future of displaced workers. Kennedy warns: "A new invention is one thing; a new invention specifically designed to get human beings out of the workplace is another."

The final article, "Back to the Future," reprinted from *National Review*, deals not only with the future of trade but also with the avoidance of "a great power war." Fareed Zakaria, the author, insists that in order to save free trade in a global economy, industrialized countries like Germany and Japan must join with the United States and address problems like environmental degradation and unemployment. First, he asserts, the U.S. must stabilize its own fiscal affairs and then initiate free trade to widen its economic base.

THE CHALLENGES AND OPPORTUNITIES OF THE GLOBAL MARKETPLACE[1]

Free Trade and International Development

I am very pleased to be the inaugural speaker for this new international business lecture series sponsored by the College of Business Administration of Georgia State University. Dean Hogan is well acquainted with my strong interest in international relations, and so I suspect he knew I would have a few opinions on the challenges and opportunities of the global marketplace.

Since I will cover a good deal of material . . . let me explain how I have organized it. I plan to go from a broad view of the international economy to a specific view of the benefits of international trade between the Southeast and Latin America. First, I will provide an overview of the economic and trade outlook for a few areas of the world — specifically the Americas, Western Europe, and the Asia-Pacific region. Next, I will briefly outline the

[1]Speech delivered by Robert P. Forrestal, president and CEO of the Federal Reserve Bank of Atlanta, on June 30, 1995, at Georgia State University, Atlanta, GA, from *Vital Speeches of the Day* 61:681–6 S 1 '95. Copyright © 1995 by City News Publishing Co. Reprinted with permission.

continuing transformation to market economies in Latin America and comment on some of the stumbling blocks this region faces as it tries to become a full partner in the global marketplace. Then I will speak about the importance of free trade and finally conclude with how the United States and the Southeast can benefit from trade with our neighbors to the south.

Before I delve into these topics, though, I would like to explain both my professional and personal interest in international affairs. First, on the professional level, as a central banker, I must pay attention to developments in other countries because the increasing expansion of world trade—as well as the globalization of financial markets—means that the Federal Reserve cannot concentrate only on domestic developments in examining the outlook for our economy. For instance, Latin America is and will be an important trading area for this nation. Developments in our trading partners influence domestic macroeconomic conditions. If growth in the gross domestic product (GDP) in other countries accelerates, U.S. exports are likely to rise. If conditions worsen in other countries, our exports typically fall.

Second, on a more personal level, the reason for my keen interest in international relations has to do with my long-held belief that free trade and international development can help to strengthen both our regional and our national economy. During my tenure as president and CEO of the Federal Reserve Bank of Atlanta, I have worked hard to expand the definition of regional economics to include international relations. If that sounds like a contradiction in terms, let me assure you that I am referring to the scope or horizon of Reserve Banks like the Atlanta Federal. To that end, our bank has promoted the idea of strong international relations by hosting lunches and dinners with the local consular corps and visiting foreign dignitaries. Last year [1994], for example, five distinguished international figures spoke at the bank to audiences of Atlanta business, academic, and community leaders. Chief among these speakers were Mary Robinson, the president of Ireland, and Raul Granillo Ocampo, the Argentine ambassador to the United States.

The Atlanta Federal has also sponsored several conferences on international themes, including one . . . on opportunities for trade and investment in Latin America and the Caribbean. In addition, since we have attracted a fair number of international visitors from central and commercial banks in countries like Peru and Russia, we have also established an Office of International Relations to coordinate these visits.

In my own way, I have tried to augment this international activity at the Atlanta Federal by accepting a few speaking engagements in other countries around the world. Earlier this month [September 1995], for example, I was in Copenhagen to deliver a talk about the role of the regional Reserve banks to policy makers at the central bank of Denmark. It seems they are anticipating the day when the European Community will have one central bank, with former central banks in each country serving more as regional Reserve banks. In the past two years, I have also had the opportunity to travel to Shanghai to discuss the development of financial markets in China and to Stockholm to discuss issues in U.S. economic policymaking. The discussions with foreign central bankers that I have had during these trips have given me very helpful insights into the larger context in which U.S. monetary policy decisions are being made.

This focus on international relations has also led me to this conclusion: In a world that is much more closely integrated economically and financially, it is absolutely necessary for all Americans to be thinking about how they fit into the world, not simply how they fit into the economy of their own country. Yes, it is difficult to understand other cultures and languages, but these hurdles should not bar the human mind from traveling great distances in order to accomplish great things. In this day and age, there are many ways to get around language barriers, and business people are business people no matter where their companies are headquartered. I cannot emphasize strongly enough how important I believe it is for the United States to be competitive in the global marketplace and for each American to understand that for every challenge in that global marketplace, there are many opportunities.

Let me now give a brief economic outlook for some of the major areas of the world, starting with that part of the world I know best, the United States. Growth in output . . . [during 1994] was 4 percent. This rate of growth was very strong relative to our potential, and the current slowing is not entirely unwelcome. Of course, that will be true only to the extent that we do not slow too much. Considering that the expansion has been going on for four years, a moderate growth rate this year of about two and a half percent on an annual average basis is absolutely appropriate and necessary. In fact, we welcome this development since we would like to ensure that current pressures on prices will prove to be a temporary and cyclical phenomenon. With growth decelerating, it is unlikely that the unemployment rate will decline much further. My best guess is that it will be close to five and a half percent on an annual average basis, but it could run above this level at times. Inflation may rise to an average of somewhat above 3 percent. It is clear that the possibility of a recession has increased given the deceleration in GDP growth, but, in my view, a recession is not the most likely outcome.

Moving on to the rest of the Americas, I can report that U.S. trade with the developing countries of our own hemisphere has skyrocketed over the last five years. From 1990 to 1994, total trade with Mexico has doubled to more than $100 billion. Trade with other developing countries in Latin America has gone from $60 billion in 1990 to $80 billion in 1994—an increase of 33 percent. Five of our fastest-growing export markets this decade are located in Latin America, and the region accounts for 15 percent of all U.S. trade.

However, . . . [1995] has been a trying year for many economies in our hemisphere, and growth in trade with Latin America will decelerate . . . . The developing nations of Latin America and the Caribbean continue to feel the effects of the Mexican financial setback that began last December [1994] when Mexican authorities let the peso depreciate. The causes of this setback may be better pursued at another forum. Nonetheless, I would like to point out that, faced with a difficult financial situation, Mexican leaders did not retreat into protectionism or nationalization as they did in the early 1980s. The fact that Mexico has enacted long-term policies designed to fix the current problem, and to prevent future ones like it, encourages me to be optimistic about the future of Mexico.

Also within the Americas region is Canada. As our single largest trading partner, it takes 22 percent of U.S. exports and ships 19 percent of U.S. imported goods. The economic outlook for Canada is very positive. Although economic growth is decelerating from the four and a half percent rate of last year [1994], Canadian real gross domestic product (GDP) should still average just under 4 percent in 1995 and 3 percent [in 1996] . . . . The slowdown should allow Canadian inflation to remain below 3 percent annually through 1996.

Looking across the Atlantic Ocean, I am pleased to see that Western Europe has cast off the last remnants of its early-1990s recession. These economies should see growth near 3 percent . . . [in 1995] as well as in 1996. U.S. trade with the European nations—which accounts for 20 percent of all U.S. trade—should pick up in the coming years. It does not seem likely that the move to incorporate more European nations into the European Union and further steps toward monetary union will have an adverse impact on U.S. trade with Europe.

Let me turn now to the third key area I would like to discuss, the Asia-Pacific region. The economy of our second-largest trading partner, Japan—which accounts for 15 percent of all U.S. trade—should stay weak through 1995, but could do better . . . if domestic demand picks up as expected. However, the benefits of financial deregulations, lower taxes, low interest rates, and increased government spending may be offset by the appreciation of the yen. Over the last year, the value of the yen has risen 12 percent compared to the currencies of major trading partners of Japan. Over the last five years, that figure is more than 80 percent. The strength of the yen is forcing many Japanese firms to slow down production or to relocate industrial facilities offshore, mainly in developing Asian countries, since products made in Japan are becoming more and more expensive overseas. This could affect corporate profits and lead to a further rise in Japanese unemployment, which would likely dampen consumer spending in Japan. After growing a scant half percent . . . [in 1994], the economy in Japan is expected to grow just over one percent . . . [for 1995] and a bit above 2 percent in 1996. Slow growth combined with trade tensions between Japan and the United States do not bode well for an increase in U.S. trade with Japan in the near future.

The economies of the developing Asian economies provide a brighter picture. I mentioned earlier that five of the top 10 fastest-growing U.S. export markets are in Latin America. The other five are found in Asia. Excluding Japan, trade with the Asian nations accounts for 20 percent of the total U.S. trade. These economies are expected to grow more than 7 percent in 1995 and 1996, down a bit from the 8 percent pace of . . . [1994]. The potential for increased U.S. trade with this region is bright because of this growth forecast and continued efforts toward freer trade taken by Asian nations.

Since I plan to comment in a few moments on the merits of increased trade with Latin America, let me go into more detail about its economic reforms. Over the past decade, Latin American nations have undergone profound economic and political change—and those changes have generally been for the better. Not too long ago, most countries in the region were beset by huge external debt burdens, rampant inflation, crushing government budget deficits, and general economic and financial malaise. In the wake of significant macroeconomic reforms, we have begun to see economic growth in a number of countries, such as Chile and Argentina. A good deal of the capital that had fled these countries in search of safer investment opportunities abroad returned—at least, before the peso shock—and foreign investment was on the rise. Democracy and free-market economies are now the norm where dictatorships and centralized economies once were. Since these have been dramatic and far-reaching changes, it would not be realistic to think that these nations could make this transition without occasional setbacks. In the long run, however, Latin America will be an increasingly important economic force in the world.

Overall, it is important to remember that the desirability of closer international economic integration has not been negated by the developments in Mexico since the end of   [1994]. It is also worth noting that, although growth in Mexico has slowed following the depreciation of the peso, other countries in Latin America are expected to continue to do well. For example, in Chile growth could reach 6 percent in 1995, up from nearly 4 percent . . . . Prudent economic policies in Chile have enabled that country to post positive rates of growth averaging 5 percent over the last decade. Inflation in Chile could fall to 8 percent . . . from nearly 9 percent in 1994. Chile has a high domestic savings rate and a financial system that is less susceptible than some of its neighbors' to destabilizing outflows of capital. Both of these attributes have helped it through the fallout from the Mexican peso depreciation. In essence, Chile is an example of a country that is benefiting from the kind of economic and political stability other Latin American nations are striving toward.

It is true that there have been problems in Latin America including the economic troubles in Mexico, the resulting effects upon foreign investment in that country and others in Latin America, and financial problems in Venezuela following the bankruptcy of its second-largest bank, Banco Latino. In addition, some Latin American countries still face serious obstacles to continuing growth, a few of which I would like to address. In my view, a lack of strong financial systems and comprehensive bank supervision is at the top of the list. I believe that the recipe for continued long-term, stable growth in Latin America—in addition to the macroeconomic policies that have already been put in place—is to have a strong financial system of well-regulated banks and an efficient payments system in place in each country. Such a financial system requires an independent central bank to ensure that the making of monetary policy is separate from fiscal decision making and is not vulnerable to political pressure by members of the government. Whether or not the bank regulatory authority is part of the central bank, it too needs to be independent to ensure that short-term political considerations do not distort and compromise the regulatory framework of the financial system.

Legal reform is another major challenge for Latin American policy makers. Among the evolving economic and political reforms taking place in many countries, one area that has not yet become firmly implanted is private property and contract law. In the industrialized world, such laws are taken for granted. However, in countries where nationalization has been a recurring theme, the concept of private property exists on shaky grounds. Setting up an enduring legal system as a foundation for newly privatized companies and property is a daunting challenge, but one that should, in my opinion, be met. Otherwise, private and corporate citizens, as well as foreign investors, will continue to operate as though the government could take their property at a moment's notice. It is in fact this very real fear of enforced nationalization that caused the extremely complex pattern of offshore holdings that developed in many Latin American countries.

A third stumbling block to market reform has to do with a lack of transparency in the financial markets of many Latin American countries. Many of you are familiar, no doubt, with the way depreciation of the Mexican peso roiled the stock markets not only in Mexico but also in Venezuela, Brazil, Argentina, Chile, and Peru. A larger issue for Latin America, though, is that events of this sort may cause foreign investors to become less willing to give Latin American countries the benefit of the doubt. I am afraid that even if the long-run fundamentals of a country are good, potential investors may worry unduly as a result of what happened in Mexico.

One source of potential help in this situation would be efforts to increase the transparency of economic and financial data for countries in Latin America. Quite simply, these countries need to increase their financial reporting. If countries want to attract capital, they need to have better measurements of both financial and nonfinancial matters. It is true that international standards of reporting are not necessarily explicit, but, at their heart, they call for well-defined data that are consistently reported and available to the public. Although such data may, at times, raise concerns about the health of a country, these same concerns would ultimately emerge even in the absence of data. By reducing uncertainty, better flows of information would likely bolster capital flows on average. Let me be clear, however, that better reporting is a burden not just for Latin American countries. The problem is even greater in Eastern European countries where business enterprises at one time reported only to their highly centralized governments.

But, in my view, it is not only reform efforts on the part of Latin American countries that will result in their transformation to market economies. I believe they need strategic help from the outside. To wit, if the United States wants to ensure that our Latin American neighbors remain on the path they have chosen, we must persist in our efforts to forge closer economic ties with them through increased trade. Expanding the North American Free Trade Agreement (NAFTA) to include other Latin American economies that have embarked on market-oriented policy reforms is a logical next step to achieve this goal. The Free Trade Area of the Americas, launched in Miami . . . during [1994], should remain a top priority for the United States.

Since I believe that free trade is the cornerstone of open-market economies, let me digress a moment to describe the long-term good brought about by free trade in general. Essentially, free trade enhances the welfare of all countries involved. People in all countries that trade freely with one another are able to purchase goods and services that would either not otherwise be available to them, or would be available only at higher cost. In addition, the production of these goods and services adds to the income of each country.

In the United States, we may have become so accustomed to the benefits of generally moderate trade barriers that we sometimes take them for granted. For instance, on the consumption side, a wide array of consumer goods—from Brazilian shoes to Chinese toys—are available at reasonable prices because U.S. tariffs are relatively low or nonexistent. On the production side, this nation has benefited from the creation of additional jobs as a result of both importing and exporting activity. Over the past twenty years, the United States has become much more export- and import-oriented. For example, imports have doubled from about 7 percent to nearly 15 percent of domestic demand, while exports have grown from about 7 percent to a little more than 12 percent of gross domestic product. The resulting increase in trade-related jobs has contributed to the overall increase in total U.S. jobs.

Free trade also allows each country to benefit from its competitive advantages with other countries in what can be described as a "win-win" situation. To understand the benefits of comparative advantage, we need only think about the concept within the context of the southeastern states. Taking the state of Georgia as an example, it clearly is wiser for Georgia not to try to produce its own citrus fruits or energy resources, such as oil, mainly because it does not have the natural attributes to do so. Georgia could develop alternative in-state supply sources through, say, the use of greenhouses or wood, but citrus fruit can more cheaply come from Florida and the energy resources can come from Louisiana.

Meanwhile, the state of Georgia has an advantage in supplying other states or parts of the world with some of the items it is good at producing, such as poultry and lumber. These examples rest—at least partly—on absolute advantages in resource availability, but the same points hold even when there is only a comparative advantage. Georgia might be quite good, even better than another state, at producing autos, but if Georgia can make paper relatively more efficiently than that other state, both are better off if Georgia concentrates on paper and the other one on autos.

In recent years, economists have increasingly recognized that comparative advantage can be based on economies of scale or agglomeration effects—not just on differences in climate or natural resources. If an industry is concentrated in a particular area, new ideas and technological advances can spread through the industry quickly. Moreover, a concentrated industry can support a variety of specialized suppliers that become highly efficient at their jobs. For example, the concentration of movie and television production in Hollywood supports an array of suppliers, from caterers who bring food to the set to film labs that edit the finished product. In the Southeast, Atlanta may be developing as a center for communications services, and Orlando is a major vacation destination with the many theme parks and attractions that have been built there.

The same logic works for countries at the global level. The United States is a leader in supplying higher value-added items, such as computer software, while other countries assemble the hardware. In the same vein, the United States does not emphasize production of videotapes but, rather, the creation of the movies that are recorded on videotapes. This comparative advantage derives from having a large group of creative, highly skilled workers. It works to the benefit of the United States because other countries that lack the numbers of such workers find it difficult to produce items such as software or movies in significant quantities, whereas it is easier for them to copy the relatively low-skill technology for assembling computer hardware or duplicating videotapes.

U.S. gains in areas that use the most technology and call for highly skilled and more educated workers have been shifting the composition of U.S. exports away from lower value-added products like food, bulk chemicals, and other commodities. In the Southeast, in contrast, such lower value-added products remain our main exports. However, low-skill, labor-intensive jobs, like many piecework jobs in the apparel industry, have been moving to other nations that have much lower-paid labor, particularly China and other Pacific-rim countries. As you would expect, the Southeast has felt the effects of this shift. Southeastern apparel employment, for example, has fallen from more than 280,000 in 1977 to less than 240,000 in 1994. As a share of manufacturing, apparel employment has declined from 13 percent to 10 percent.

As hard as this process of change may be on some communities in the Southeast and nation that once relied on industries like apparel as a main source of employment and income, it must be remembered that this course of events is natural for a dynamic, wealthy country like the United States. Clearly it makes no sense for the wealthiest nation in the world to try to sustain certain industries simply to keep low-paying jobs within our borders. We are ultimately better off creating the kinds of products and services whose added value is higher and heightens our comparative advantage in the world.

This process of change, however, cannot happen overnight. It involves raising the educational level of all Americans so that an increasing number will possess the education and skills needed in the production of higher value-added items. Unfortunately, in the South our investment in primary and secondary education, as opposed to higher education, has historically lagged behind the rest of the nation, and this lag represents a serious stumbling block in our bid to continue long-term growth and to expand exports. This is not a new argument in regard to the South, but it cannot be ignored in the face of mounting pressure to compete not only with other regions in the United States but also with other countries in the world.

In areas of the country where low-skill, low-wage jobs are common, as in the South, so, too, is sentiment toward protectionism. Therefore, it is particularly important to increase understanding about how free trade benefits those countries involved over the long run. There is still a widespread view that trade is essentially static; in other words, it is frequently thought of as a zero-sum game. Too often we hear international trade discussed in terms of job losses, forgetting that jobs are also created through trade. In fact, trade is dynamic. The more trade there is, the larger the pie gets, with the result that no country loses in the long term. Consider Mexico and NAFTA, for example. Even though that country is currently dealing with economic problems stemming from the depreciation of the peso against the dollar, over time the new system of free trade will allow Mexicans to create more jobs. Higher income from these jobs will enable Mexican workers to purchase more U.S. goods and services. In the long run, both countries will be better off.

These lessons about free trade apply not only to Europe and Japan, with whom we are already trading on a large scale, but also to Latin America. For this reason, it is encouraging to see the great strides made toward market economies in Latin America because the resulting stronger economies also create more opportunities for trade.

But what exactly are the implications for the United States and the Southeast? At the most fundamental level, as I have mentioned, the result will be more jobs—jobs in the United States and jobs in Latin America, all tied to increased trade. According to the Commerce Department, U.S. manufacturing exports to the world increased by 95 percent in the period between 1987 and 1993, whereas they increased by 138 percent to Latin America and the Caribbean. Argentina, Chile, Colombia, and Mexico saw the greatest increases in manufacturing imports from the United States during that period. Unlike the vicious cycle of retaliation that protectionism leads to, free trade is a virtuous cycle that creates jobs and makes all countries better off.

Once the benefits of free trade are recognized, the next question is where the United States and, in particular, the Southeast, should focus its exporting efforts. Proximity is one of the characteristics of enduring trading partners, and the current experience of the United States bears this out, since Canada is our No. 1 export market and Mexico has been close behind second-place Japan, whose economy is much larger. Thus, from a purely geographical point of view, trade with our neighbors to the south makes good sense.

But there are other reasons to focus trade efforts on Latin America. From the point of view of the United States, we are better off when our neighbors to the south as well as to the north are thriving economically— thus increasing their imports from us—rather than deteriorating. In view of the current problems in Mexico, it may seem that now is not the right time to be recommending that the United States and the Southeast look southward for trade opportunities. But one must take the long view when thinking about trade, and in the long view the focus should return to the positive fundamentals of the Latin American economies and the enormous potential they hold.

Right now, the developing economies, in particular Latin America and Asia, are growing faster than our largest trading partners—Western Europe and Japan. As Latin Americans have more money to spend on products and services from the United States, it seems very likely that U.S. export shares will continue to increase to this and other growing regions of the world. The Southeast can take advantage of this increased trade by focusing on products most likely to be needed by emerging market economies: capital equipment, commercial services, and consumer goods.

. . . We are in . . . an economic expansion since the 1990–91 recession, the strength of the economic recovery in much of the Southeast has cemented the reputation of the region as a full partner—if not a leader—in the national economy. In fact, this region of the country has been outperforming the United States in job growth for a number of years, with the nation playing catch-up.

In particular, we in the South need not bow to any other region of this nation when it comes to being able to work with international visitors. We have been leaders in understanding the importance of the international economy to the economic well-being of the region. For instance, long before economic developers in other parts of the nation began to think internationally, Southerners—led by those in North and South Carolina—were already laying the groundwork and attracting European investors. The early result in the 1970s was that of all the foreign industrial development in the nation, half was being put into the South. Now we have German and Japanese car makers as well as Dutch, Irish, and British manufacturers, to name just a few. I might add that all of the marketing that is being done in the name of the Olympics can only increase the desirability of locating in the Southeast for international companies.

Early in the recovery following the 1990–91 recession, the Southeast was "fast out of the gate," so to speak, thanks to the upsurge in home building throughout the nation and the region's concentration in building-related industries and durable goods manufacturing. For instance, much of the lumber, carpeting, and appliances needed to build and furnish new homes comes from the Southeast. Building on these successes, it is in the best interest of the region that its economy should continue to evolve and diversify.

Over the past few decades, the Southeast relied heavily for its growth on attracting companies from other parts of the United States with its warmer climate, lower wages, weaker unions, and lower taxes. However, most of the firms that could make such moves have already done so, and it is time for the region to move on to new strategies for further development. Through trade with other countries, we can promote further growth of the industries that are now well established in our region as well as the development of new industries. The happy consequence of such exports will be a greater diversification of the southeastern economy.

In reality, though, the opportunity for exporting may not have been fully tapped in the Southeast in that, as measured by the share of jobs that is export-based, the region does some 20 percent less exporting than the United States as a whole. Moreover, given that the Southeast tends to export more lower value-added products than does the nation, the region faces certain problems. For instance, exports such as bulk chemicals and certain paper products put some areas of the Southeast in the same league as a developing nation, compared with other regions of the United States that export more high value-added items, such as machine tools, transportation equipment, and electronics.

Exactly how does the Southeast stand to benefit by increasing trade with Latin America? Before the depreciation of the peso in Mexico, the region had significantly increased its trade of poultry and commodities to that country. Although common wisdom has it that the volume of these exports should fall off due to the depreciation of the peso, it is difficult to say whether—or to what extent—income from them will fall. Tourism has also traditionally been something that this region has exported, in a manner of speaking. When people from abroad come to the many theme parks in Florida, we are really exporting a service, albeit primarily to Canada and Western Europe. However, Latin Americans are the fastest growing group of tourists visiting Florida. Another area that has been buoyed by foreign demand is housing, particularly in Miami where Latin Americans who are doing business have been buying homes in increasing numbers.

Now that NAFTA is in place, the question for business people is, what should the Southeast be trading to Latin America in the future? Statistics from the Inter-American Development Bank indicate that, for exports to Argentina, Brazil, Chile, and Mexico over the last five years, the fastest-growing value-added areas were construction, transportation, communications, utilities, financial services, and wholesale and retail trade. Some of these are industries in which businesses in the Southeast have a comparative advantage—and many have already begun to do more trading with Latin American countries.

In conclusion, international trade should continue to be a strong avenue of growth for the Southeast and its businesses. We must understand that free trade with Latin America, and the rest of the world for that matter, is not a threat to our economy. Instead, it is an opportunity waiting to be captured by businesses in the Southeast. I can think of few better ways to step up to meet the challenges and opportunities in the global marketplace than to set our sights on increased trade with our friends and neighbors to the south.

FROM GATT TO WTO: THE INSTITUTIONALIZATION OF WORLD TRADE[2]

Over the past few decades, a system of relatively open exchange, particularly in merchandise trade, has prevailed in the world under the auspices of the General Agreement on Tariffs and Trade (GATT). Today, most economists acknowledge this trading system as one of the greatest contributors to the world's rapid recovery from the desolation of World War II, and to the phenomenal growth in world output thereafter. Through all of those years, however, GATT has served its member countries through a loose and informal structure, with all the inevitable problems that accompany a weak and ill-defined authority. With the passage of the Uruguay Round of trade talks, this trading system is poised to take on a new shape in a permanent institution known as the World Trade Organization (WTO). Although much skepticism and controversy have surrounded the birth of WTO, it is the hope of all free-traders that the new WTO will be able to amend what went amiss with GATT.

A Brief History of Trade

At the beginning of the nineteenth century, economists began to make advances in interpreting why human beings had always engaged in economic exchange. The theory of comparative advantage posited that countries specialize in those goods and services that they can produce more efficiently relative to other countries. When nations concentrate their production on commodities in which they have a comparative advantage, consumers

[2]Article by Salil S. Pitroda, staff writer, from *Harvard International Review* 17:46+ Ap 1 '95.

as a whole benefit from lower prices and a greater range of consumption possibilities. Because each good is produced by the country that is best at producing it, scarce world resources are allocated efficiently. Like all economic activities, the distribution of the benefits of trade is not uniform; yet in general and in the long run, trade leads to a more optimal economic outcome with greater competition and greater productivity—a rising tide on which all boats float.

In 1947, such a view of the benefits of international cooperation inspired a group of visionaries gathered in Bretton Woods, NH, to erect a new economic world order from the ravages of World War II. The Bretton Woods Accords, which celebrated their fiftieth anniversary . . . [in 1994], established the World Bank and the International Monetary Fund and led to the creation of GATT. These structures, albeit not always true to the visionary spirit in which they were founded, have formed the underpinnings of world economic development for the past half century.

GATT has become the framework for international trade in our time. The body was formed as an interim secretariat for trade negotiations after the United States, bowing to protectionist sentiment, refused to ratify the charter of the stillborn International Trade Organization, a full-fledged institution of the stature of the World Bank and the IMF. Based in Geneva and currently encompassing over 190 member nations, GATT has acted as a conduit for multilateral negotiations on a variety of international trade issues, including tariff and quota policy and trading practices. It has sponsored several rounds of protracted, though eventually fruitful, trade talks where members gathered to hammer out the details of the set of rules governing economic exchange. GATT panels make recommendations on changes in trade regulations and review complaints against member countries.

Despite GATT's success in coordinating international trade policy, it must be remembered that GATT is only an interim body without a fully defined institutional structure and with little legal enforcement power. For instance, many loopholes exist in the mechanism dealing with disputes regarding unfair trade practices. If a country complains of unfair trading practices on the part of another country and a GATT panel concurs with the complaint, the accused country can dissent from the finding, effectively vetoing it and preventing the complaining country from retaliation within the GATT framework. Another increasingly popular way of doing business in an extra-GATT environment is through the creation of regional trade blocs, such as the European Union (EU), the North American Free Trade Agreement (NAFTA) and the impending Association of Southeast Asian Nations (ASEAN) free trade agreement. These regional agreements, in effect, set their own rules of trade, encouraging cooperative exchange within a bloc but hinting of protectionism against countries outside the region. Non-tariff trade barriers (NTBs), such as a German requirement that, for health reasons, beer sold in Germany be made with German water, are also another device for bending GATT rules. Another way of eschewing GATT policy through these regional trading arrangements is to manipulate the rules of origin stipulation. By raising the requirement of local content value, aspiring profiteers and vested interests can turn an ostensible reduction in a tariff into an actual increase by subjecting formerly tariff-exempt goods to duties, thus circumventing the GATT guideline that for any free trade agreement the new common external tariff be no higher than the average tariff of the constituent states before the accord. Without any institutional framework or legal authority, the most that GATT can do, when confronted with such adroit legerdemain with its regulations, is to urge and exhort a spirit of cooperation among member states, each of whom has an individual incentive to cater to local interests by eschewing a rule here and raising a protectionist wall there.

Seeking to address some of these problems, the Uruguay Round of negotiations was launched nearly nine years ago. Under the leadership of GATT Director-General Peter Sutherland, this latest round of trade talks has arrived at a consensus on implementing changes to the international framework that will encourage greater openness and trade integration among the world's nations. First and foremost, the Uruguay Round promises a lowering of trade barriers and a slashing of tariffs by an average of one-third. It broadens the scope of liberalization to include traditionally protected industries such as textiles and apparel. Reflecting the changing nature of world trade, the Uruguay Round will open up exchange in the previously closed but rapidly emerging areas of agriculture, services, and intellectual property. It imposes a new discipline on NTBs and government procurement and offers clarification on subsidies, dumping regulations, quota restrictions and voluntary export restraints. It also lays the foundation for further talks dealing with important trade issues including the treatment of foreign direct investment, labor and environmental concerns, and capital and currency market fluctuations. Most importantly, the Uruguay Round of accords has boldly moved the world a step closer to global free trade by calling for the establishment of the WTO to succeed the GATT secretariat.

The Birth of WTO

The WTO will be a new international institution, on par with the World Bank and the IMF, that will outline a framework for all areas of international trade and will have the legal authority to settle trade disputes. In legal terms, it represents the maturation of the GATT secretariat into a full-fledged, permanent international entity. The supreme decision-making body will be a biannual ministerial meeting, affording the organization more political clout and a higher international profile. This WTO council will then have subsidiary working bodies that specialize in areas of trade including goods, services, and intellectual property. Unlike GATT, the WTO will have a clearly defined dispute settlement mechanism. Independent panel reports will automatically be adopted by the WTO council unless there is a clear consensus to reject them. Countries who are accused of engaging in unfair trade practices can appeal to a permanent appellate body, but the verdict of this body will be ultimately binding. If an offending nation fails to comply with WTO panel recommendations, its trading partners will be guaranteed the right to compensation as determined by the panel or, as a final resort, be given the right to impose countervailing sanctions. All members of the WTO will have legal access to these multilateral dispute settlement mechanisms, and all stages of WTO deliberation will be time-limited, ensuring efficiency in dispute settlement. The World Trade Organization will be akin to an International Court of Justice for world trade, with the institutional strength and legal mandate to ensure fair trade and global economic integration.

Who will be the pioneering leader of this newly constructed international organization? The ideal candidate must possess a strategic global vision of world trade while being comfortable with technical complexity. He or she must combine the finesse of a diplomat, the organizational acumen of an experienced administrator and the leadership qualities of a seasoned statesman.

Since Peter Sutherland, the incumbent Director-General of GATT has indicated his wish to stand down in favor of fresh leadership, the competition to be the head of the WTO has been opened up to three dynamic candidates. Renato Ruggiero, the favored candidate of the EU, is a former trade minister of Italy and has also been suggested in the past as a possible president of the European Commission. He has emphasized his experience as a capable administrator with international experience in Brussels, the GATT, and world economic summits. Carlos Salinas de Gortari, who during his tenure as the President of Mexico defined the paradigm for economic liberalization in developing countries, is the candidate favored by the Americas. His international stature as a head of state and his commitment to free trade—as evinced by his personal crusade for NAFTA—are Salinas's most important assets. The South Korean trade minister, Kim Chul-Su, has proven international experience and is naturally supported by countries in Asia and Australia, the fastest growing region in the world. In the end, politics will most likely decide who heads the WTO. Similar leadership positions are opening up at the Organization for Economic Cooperation and Development (OECD) and other international organizations, with political horse-trading sure to play an integral role in determining the new leaders of these organizations.

There are various other strategic issues relating to the establishment of the WTO. At least for the initial transition stage, the new organization is expected to grow by expanding on the existing GATT structure. The WTO will most probably be situated in the existing GATT building in Geneva and will require an increase in GATT's present budget and staff. Yet even with this augmentation in resources, the WTO will still remain far smaller in size than either the World Bank or the IMF.

Aside from such logistical matters, however, the precise nature of the transition between GATT and WTO remains more nebulous. Some countries, such as the United States, have already announced that they will terminate their GATT membership within sixty days of joining the WTO. Such a strict view of WTO's successor status to GATT raises interesting questions about U.S. obligations to GATT members who have yet to ratify their entry into WTO.

Other countries envision the two organizations operating in tandem for a period of two years, with GATT still binding, to ease the transition to the WTO. There is also the question of new memberships. Will Slovenia and Croatia, for instance, who have just applied for GATT membership, be granted direct membership in the WTO? If the WTO does not completely supersede GATT immediately, where does that leave a country like the Sudan, which is not a GATT member, but has applied directly for WTO membership?

Of course, there is also the thorny problem of China, which has just been denied the opportunity of being a founding member of WTO, and Taiwan, whose competing applications will surely pose more dilemmas of politics and protocol. Certainly, careful deliberation will be needed to work out the multitude of implementational, organizational, and transitional issues.

The Foundation of the New Order

Given these birth pangs, what are the fundamental qualities upon which the WTO must lay its foundation? As Carlos Salinas de Gortari has outlined in a recent article in *The Financial Times*, the WTO must be representative, reliable, and responsive. It must embrace all countries, regardless of their level of economic development, and ensure their prompt and satisfactory integration into a multilateral trading system. Reliability is a much tougher criterion to satisfy. The WTO must clarify GATT rules, broaden its mandate and improve its dispute settlement mechanisms to demonstrate to all member nations that they have a stake in abiding by a rules-based trade regime. Finally, flexibility and responsiveness to the evolving changes of the international economy will ensure that the WTO retains the political support necessary to carrying out its work.

As an organization that has ambitions of leading the global economy into the next millennium, the WTO needs to legitimize its standing in the eyes of politicians and economists wearied by decades of trade negotiations by confronting some concrete and difficult problems. One of the first tasks it might have to face is deciding whether or not it should extend the rules regulating conduct in international trade to cover national competition policies. Ideally, countries should have roughly comparable standards on anti-trust legislation so that greater competition from all-comers, whether domestic or foreign, can be welcomed. But by treading on such sensitive territories, the WTO may stray too far from the trade-related issues at the core of its mandate. The animosities which it incurs in those confrontations may permanently impair its ability to unite its membership on other, arguably even more important, issues in the long run.

One of the most crucial tasks of the WTO will be presiding over the economic and political integration of the former socialist economies. It must provide stable and expanding outlets for these countries' products to encourage the liberalization of their economies and to help them attract much needed foreign direct investment. In fact, all the newly open economies in Latin America, Africa, and Asia must be nurtured by a transparent, rules-based, and mutually beneficial trading system. In particular, the WTO must encourage the reversal of the growing lethargy in North-South cooperation, especially with regard to Sub-Saharan African countries, which desperately need open international markets for their growth. The organization also has a special responsibility to bring the nearly two billion citizens of China and India, 40 percent of the planet's population, into the world trading regime as full and active members.

On a more macroscopic level, the WTO must effectively coordinate regional free trade agreements to ensure that they do not conflict in goals or create islands of protectionism, but are instead regional building blocks toward the eventual realization of global free trade which almost every economic theory praises as the ideal for future world economic relations. Pursuant to this objective of regional coordination, the institution must stiffen its regulations and their enforcement so that less and less protectionism can be veiled behind devices such as NTBs, rules of origins requirements, and other technical loopholes. It must convince member nations that their greatest economic interest is to cooperate with the other nations of the world and not bow to vested interests by taking short-sighted unilateral action. The best means for guaranteeing this end is a vigorous and binding dispute settlement mechanism. In planning for the future, the organization must also proactively embrace the changing nature of the global economy from trade in manufactured goods to trade in information-intensive services and intellectual property. The technical complexity of those issues and the administrative difficulty that will inevitably accompany any rules governing them will be a challenge to WTO's energy, resourcefulness, and resolve.

Finally, and very importantly, the WTO must acknowledge and deal with some of the local pains that uncompetitive industries in member nations will feel. In order to avoid the image of an elitist other-worldliness to which so many other well-intentioned international organizations have fallen prey, the WTO must ensure that the gains from trade are trickled down to the populace. Without at least some semblance of equity to compensate for the sacrifices that the working poor will be asked to make in any transition, it will be difficult for WTO to maintain the political and moral support that it needs to push through its vision of world-wide free trade. Ideally, some sort of structural adjustment fund and a common program for retraining displaced workers should be a pillar of the WTO, so that humanity and compassion, as well as hard-nosed efficiency, may be integrated into the organization's founding philosophy. There are undoubtedly a host of other important issues the new WTO should consider, but careful deliberation upon the fundamentals outlined here will be a major step toward solidifying and validating a global free trade system.

Positive Sums from Cooperation

The bottom line of the emergence of the new WTO from GATT is that world trade will be institutionalized in the formal legal structure of an international organization. The more formal status of the WTO will allow it to give more focus and publicity to efforts that attempt to create greater global cooperation in international trade. The institutionalization of trade through the WTO will give some bite to the bark of a well-articulated set of trading rules and policies. With its creation, there will exist an independent political entity that can view the world trading system from a holistic perspective and to check and balance competing interests that seek to bend the trading rules in their national or sectoral favor. By paying judicious attention to the fundamental issues in international trade, the WTO has the potential of becoming a visionary organization that outlines a bold path for international trade and leads the world into a new economic renaissance.

Recent studies have released estimates of the global economic effects of the ratification of the GATT Uruguay Round and the creation of the World Trade Organization. A GATT report re-

leased in November 1994 prognosticated that implementation of
the Uruguay Round will spur an increase of $510 billion a year
in world income by the year 2005. This figure is a vast underesti-
mate, for it does not account for the impact of strengthened procedures and rules in the services trade or better dispute
settlement mechanisms. Breaking up the gains by region, the report predicted that by 2005 the annual income gain will be $122
billion for the United States, $164 billion for the European
Union, $27 billion for Japan and $116 billion for the developing
and transitional socialist economies as a group. Figures estimat-
ing the increase in volume in the goods trade range from nine to
24 percent once the liberalization of the Uruguay Round comes
into effect. In 1992 dollars, this gain represents an increase in
trade flows of upwards of $670 billion. The report also suggests
that Uruguay Round provisions for developing and transition
economies will have the intended result of encouraging rapid
growth, as exports and imports from this group are likely to be
50 percent over and beyond the increase for the rest of the world
as a whole. The economic impact of a well-structured and credible institutionalization of international trade is likely to be enormous.

What remains to be done is the actual construction of this economic structure. Nowhere has the debate over GATT and the
WTO been more pronounced than in the world's economic leader, the United States. As is to be expected before embarking
upon any bold new initiative, those who stand to suffer short-
term losses are trying to stand in the way of long-term progress.
Protectionist concerns and irresponsible exaggeration have been
vociferously fed to the press and the deliberative bodies of the
government. One example of such red herrings is a concern
about a loss of U.S. sovereignty in becoming a member of the
WTO. In truth, any changes in the law of the United States or
any other nation will have to be ratified by proper legislative bodies in that country, and so the practical encroachment on national
sovereignty is little more than negligible. Of course, there is a
germ of truth in this argument, for when any nation enters into
an international treaty, it must lose some "sovereignty" to the extent that it agrees to abide by the terms of the agreement. Some
kind of consensus, such as the sensitive balance that needs to be
achieved by the WTO, must be reached to preserve a predictable
and liberal international trade regime. To carp at the WTO for

having the potential to compromise national sovereignty is little different from saying that national sovereignty is compromised because a country has to abide by any international treaty.

All nations, the U.S. in particular, must realize that partnerships are more advantageous than going it alone, and that economic cooperation is not a zero-sum game. Free trade makes each and every nation more prosperous because it makes the entire world more prosperous. Government leaders around the world would do well to hearken to the words of Rufus Yerxa, Deputy U.S. Trade Representative and Ambassador to GATT: "International cooperation will bring about the economic growth of the future. We cannot survive as an island in a sea of change. If we don't embrace this change, it will be our enemy rather than our friend. Cooperation is in our own self-interest."

DUTCH TULIPS AND EMERGING MARKETS[3]

Another Bubble Bursts

During the first half of the 1990s, both economic and political events in developing countries defied all expectations. Nations that most thought would not regain access to world financial markets for a generation abruptly became favorites of private investors, who plied them with capital inflows on a scale not seen since before World War I. Governments that had spent half a century pursuing statist, protectionist policies suddenly got free market religion. It was, it seemed to many observers, the dawn of a new golden age for global capitalism.

To some extent the simultaneous reversals in government policies and investor sentiment were the result of external factors. Low interest rates in the advanced countries encouraged investors to look again at opportunities in the Third World; the fall of communism not only helped to discredit statist policies everywhere but reassured investors that their assets in the developing

[3]Article by Paul R. Krugman, professor of Economics at Stanford University, from *Foreign Affairs* 74:28–44 Jl 1 '95. Copyright © 1995 by Council on Foreign Relations. Reprinted with permission.

world were unlikely to be seized by leftist governments. Still, probably the most important factor in the new look of developing countries was a sea change in the intellectual Zeitgeist: the almost universal acceptance, by governments and markets alike, of a new view about what it takes to develop.

This new view has come to be widely known as the "Washington consensus," a phrase coined by John Williamson of the Institute for International Economics. By "Washington" Williamson meant not only the U.S. government, but all those institutions and networks of opinion leaders centered in the world's de facto capital—the International Monetary Fund, World Bank, think tanks, politically sophisticated investment bankers, and worldly finance ministers, all those who meet each other in Washington and collectively define the conventional wisdom of the moment.

Williamson's original definition of the Washington consensus involved ten different aspects of economic policy. One may, however, roughly summarize this consensus, at least as it influenced the beliefs of markets and governments, more simply. It is the belief that Victorian virtue in economic policy—free markets and sound money—is the key to economic development. Liberalize trade, privatize state enterprises, balance the budget, peg the exchange rate, and one will have laid the foundations for an economic takeoff; find a country that has done these things, and there one may confidently expect to realize high returns on investments.

To many people the rise of the Washington consensus seemed to mark a fundamental turning point in world economic affairs. Now that the dead hand of the state was being lifted from Third World economies, now that investors were becoming aware of the huge possibilities for profit in these economies, the world was set for a prolonged period of rapid growth in hitherto poor countries and massive capital flows from North to South. The question was not whether optimistic expectations about growth in the big emerging markets would be fulfilled; it was whether advanced countries would be able to cope with the new competition and take advantage of the opportunities this growth now offered.

And then came the Mexican crisis. The country that was widely regarded as a model for the new regime—a once-protectionist nation that had not only greatly lowered its trade barriers but actually signed a free trade pact with the United

States, whose economic policy was run by articulate American-trained technocrats, and which had emerged from seven lean years of debt crisis to attract capital inflows on a scale unimaginable a few years earlier was once again appealing for emergency loans. But what is the meaning of Mexico's tail-spin? Is it merely the product of specific Mexican blunders and political events, or does it signal the unsoundness of the whole emerging market boom of the previous five years?

Many claim that Mexico's problems carry few wider implications. On one side, they argue that a currency crisis says more about short-term monetary management than about long-run development prospects. And to some extent they are clearly right. Currency crises are so similar to one another that they are a favorite topic for economic theorists, who lovingly detail the unchanging logic by which the collision between domestic goals and an unsustainable exchange rate generates a sudden, massive speculative attack. The December 1994 attack on the peso looked a lot like the September 1992 attack on the pound sterling, which looked quite similar to the 1973 and 1971 attacks on the dollar and the 1969 run on gold. So perhaps one should not draw broad conclusions from the fact that a developing country has managed to make the same mistakes that nearly every advanced country has made at some time in the past.

On the other side, defenders of the Washington consensus point to the many uniquely Mexican aspects of the current crisis. Certainly the combination of peasant uprisings, mysterious assassinations, and bizarre fraternal intrigue has no close counterpart anywhere else in the world.

And yet Mexico's crisis is neither a temporary setback nor a purely Mexican affair. Something like that crisis was an accident waiting to happen because the stunning initial success of the Washington consensus was based not on solid achievements, but on excessively optimistic expectations. The point is not that the policy recommendations that Williamson outlined are wrong, but that their efficacy—their ability to turn Argentina into Taiwan overnight—was greatly oversold. Indeed, the five-year reign of the Washington consensus may usefully be thought of as a sort of speculative bubble—one that involved not only the usual economic process by which excessive market optimism can be a temporarily self-fulfilling prophecy, but a more subtle political process through which the common beliefs of policymakers and investors proved mutually reinforcing. Unfortunately, any such self-reinforcing process unfortunately must eventually be faced with a reality check, and if the reality is not as good as the myth, the bubble bursts. For all its special features, the Mexican crisis marks the beginning of the deflation of the Washington consensus. That deflation ensures that the second half of the 1990s will be a far more problematic period for global capitalism than the first.

The Real Payoff to Reform

Economists have, of course, long preached the virtues of free markets. The economic case for free trade in particular, while not completely watertight, is far stronger than most people imagine. The logic that says that tariffs and import quotas almost always reduce real income is deep and has survived a century and a half of often vitriolic criticism nearly intact. And experience teaches that governments that imagine or pretend that their interventionist strategies are a sophisticated improvement on free trade nearly always turn out, on closer examination, to be engaged in largely irrational policies—or worse, in policies that are rational only in the sense that they benefit key interest groups at the expense of everyone else.

Yet there is a dirty little secret in international trade analysis. The measurable costs of protectionist policies—the reductions in real income that can be attributed to tariffs and import quotas—are not all that large. The costs of protection, according to the textbook models, come from the misallocation of resources: protectionist economies deploy their capital and labor in industries in which they are relatively inefficient, instead of concentrating on those industries in which they are relatively efficient, exporting those products in exchange for the rest. These costs are very real, but when you try to add them up, they are usually smaller than the rhetoric of free trade would suggest. For example, most estimates of the cost of protection in the United States put it well under one percent of GDP. Even that cost is largely due to the United States' preference for policies, like its sugar import quota, that generate high profits for those foreign suppliers granted access to the U.S. market. Highly protected economies, like most developing countries before the rise of the Washington consensus, suffer more. Still, conventional estimates of the costs of protection have rarely exceeded five percent of GDP. That is, the standard estimates suggest that a highly protectionist developing country, by moving to completely free trade, would get a one-time economic boost equal to the growth China achieves every five or six months.

Admittedly, many economists argue that the adverse effects of protection are larger, and thus the growth boost from trade liberalization is greater, than such conventional estimates suggest. Roughly speaking, they have suggested three mechanisms. First, protection reduces competition in the domestic market. The monopoly power that is created for domestic firms that no longer face foreign competition may be reflected either in slack management or, if a small number of firms are trying to secure monopoly positions, in wasteful duplication. Second, protectionist policies—and other policies like interest rate controls—create profits that accrue to whoever is influential enough to receive the appropriate government licenses. In a well-known paper, Anne Krueger, who later became the chief economist at the World Bank, argued that in many developing countries, the resources squandered in pursuit of these profits represent a larger net cost to the economy than the distortion that protectionism causes in the industrial mix. Finally, many people have argued that protectionism discourages innovation and the introduction of new products, thereby having sustained effects on growth that a static estimate misses. The important point about these arguments for large gains from trade liberalization, however, is that they are all fairly speculative; one cannot say as a matter of principle that these effects of protection discourage growth. It is an empirical question.

And the empirical evidence for huge gains from free market policies is, at best, fuzzy. There have been a number of attempts to measure the benefits of free trade by comparing countries. An influential 1987 study by the World Bank classified forty-one developing countries as "closed" (protectionist) or "open" and concluded that openness was associated with substantially stronger growth. But such studies have often been critiqued for using subjective criteria in deciding which countries have freer trade; the decision to class South Korea as "open," for example, has raised many doubts. A survey by UCLA's Sebastian Edwards concluded that studies which purport to show that countries with liberal trade regimes systematically grow more rapidly than those with closed markets "have been plagued by empirical and conceptual shortcomings that have resulted, in many cases, in unconvincing results whose fragility has been exposed by subsequent work."

There are surely additional gains to reforming economies from domestic liberalization, privatization, and so on. These gains have not been as thoroughly studied as those from trade liberalization. They are, however, conceptually very similar, and there is no reason to expect them to be dramatically larger or to change the picture of real but limited gains from reform.

All this does not mean that trade liberalization is not a good idea. It almost certainly is. Nor does it necessarily mean that the modest conventional estimates of the gains from such liberalization tell the whole story. But it does mean that the widespread belief that moving to free trade and free markets will produce a dramatic acceleration in a developing country's growth represents a leap of faith, rather than a conclusion based on hard evidence.

What about the other half of the Washington consensus, the belief in the importance of sound money? Here the case is even weaker.

If standard estimates of the costs of protection are lower than you might expect, such estimates of the cost of inflation—defined as the overall reduction in real income—are so low that they are embarrassing. Of course very high inflation rates—the triple- or quadruple-digit inflations that have, unfortunately, been all too common in Latin American history—seriously disrupt the functioning of a market economy. But it is very difficult to pin down any large gains from a reduction in the inflation rate from, say, 20 percent to 2 percent.

Moreover, the methods used to achieve disinflation in developing countries—above all, the use of a pegged exchange rate as a way to build credibility—have serious costs. A country with an inflationary history that tries to end inflation by establishing a fixed exchange rate almost always finds that the momentum of inflation continues for a considerable time, throwing domestic costs and prices out of line with the rest of the world. Thus an exchange rate that initially seemed reasonable usually seems considerably overvalued by the time inflation finally subsides. Furthermore, an exchange rate that is tolerable when introduced may become difficult to sustain when world market conditions change, such as the price of oil, the value of the dollar, and interest rates. Textbook international economics treats the decision about whether to fix a country's exchange rate as a difficult trade-off, which even countries committed to low inflation often end up resolving on the side of exchange rate flexibility.

Nonetheless, during the first half of the 1990s a number of developing countries adopted rigid exchange rate targets. (The most extreme case was Argentina, which established a supposedly permanent one-for-one exchange rate between the peso and the U.S. dollar). In large part this was a move designed to restore credibility after the uncontrolled inflation of the 1980s. Nonetheless, both governments and markets seem to have convinced themselves that the painful tradeoffs traditionally involved in such a commitment no longer applied.

The Dismal Cycle

In sum, then, a cool-headed analysis of the likely effects of the economic reforms undertaken in developing countries in recent years did not and does not seem to justify wild enthusiasm. Trade liberalization and other moves to free up markets are almost surely good things, but the idea that they will generate a growth take-off represents a hope rather than a well-founded expectation. Bringing down inflation is also a good thing, but doing so by fixing the exchange rate brings a mixture of benefits and costs, with the arguments against as strong as the arguments for. And yet the behavior of both governments and markets during the last five years does not suggest that they took any such measured view. On the contrary, governments eagerly adopted Washington consensus reform packages, while markets enthusiastically poured funds into reforming economies. Why?

Everyone is familiar with the way that a speculative bubble can develop in a financial market. Investors, for whatever reason, come to take a more favorable view of the prospects for some traded asset Deutsche marks, Japanese stocks, shares in the South Sea Company, tulip futures. This leads to a rise in the asset's price. If investors then interpret this gain as a trend rather than a one-time event, they become still more anxious to buy the asset, leading to a further rise, and so on. In principle, long-sighted investors are supposed to prevent such speculative bubbles by selling assets that have become overpriced or buying them when they have become obviously cheap. Sometimes, however, markets lose sight of the long run, especially when the long run is complex or obscure. Thus speculative bubbles in soybean futures tend to be limited by the common knowledge that a lot more soybeans will be grown if the price gets very high. But the chain of events that must eventually end a speculative bubble in, say, the mark—an overvalued mark reduces German exports, leading to a weak German economy, so the Bundesbank reduces interest rates, making it unattractive to hold mark-denominated assets—is often too long and abstract to seem compelling to investors when the herd is running.

It seems fairly clear that some of the enthusiasm for investing in developing countries in the first half of the 1990s was a classic speculative bubble. A modest recovery in economic prospects from the dismal 1980s led to large capital gains for those few investors who had been willing to put money into Third World stock markets. Their success led other investors to jump in, driving prices up still further. And by 1993 or so "emerging market funds" were being advertised on television and the pages of popular magazines.

At the same time that this self-reinforcing process was under way in the financial markets, a different kind of self-reinforcing process, sociological rather than economic, was taking place in the world of affairs—the endless rounds of meetings, speeches, and exchanges of communiques that occupy much of the time of economic opinion leaders. Such interlocking social groupings tend at any given time to converge on a conventional wisdom, about economics among many other things. People believe certain stories because everyone important tells them, and people tell those stories because everyone important believes them. Indeed, when a conventional wisdom is at its fullest strength, one's agreement with that conventional wisdom becomes almost a litmus test of one's suitability to be taken seriously.

Anyone who tried, two or three years ago, to express even mild skepticism about the prospects for developing countries knows how difficult it was to make any impression on either business or political leaders. Views contrary to the immense optimism of the time were treated not so much with hostility as bemusement. How could anyone be so silly as to say these gloomy things?

While both a speculative bubble in the financial markets and the standard process whereby influential people rally around a conventional wisdom surely played a role in the astonishing rise of the Washington consensus, there was, however, an additional, distinctive self-reinforcing process that arguably played an even greater role. This was a political economy cycle, in which governments were persuaded to adopt Washington consensus policies because markets so spectacularly rewarded them, and in which markets were willing to supply so much capital because they thought they saw an unstoppable move toward policy reform.

One must begin with a key insight of Dani Rodrik of Columbia University. Rodrik pointed out that economists and international organizations like the World Bank had been arguing for a long time in favor of freer trade in developing countries. The intellectual case for protectionism to promote industrialization, while popular in the 1950s, has been pretty much moribund since the late 1960s. Nonetheless, the stake of established interest groups in the existing system blocked any major move to free trade. When limited liberalization was attempted, it usually ended up being abandoned a few years later. Why did this suddenly change?

One seemingly obvious answer is the Third World debt crisis of the 1980s, which made the previous system untenable. But economic crises, especially when they involve the balance of payments, traditionally lead to more protectionism, not less. Why was this case different?

Rodrik's answer was that in the 1990s, advocates of free trade in developing countries were able to link free trade to financial and macroeconomic benefits. If trade liberalization is presented as a detailed microeconomic policy, the industries that stand to lose will be well-informed and vociferous in their opposition, while those who stand to gain will be diffuse and ineffective. What reformers in a number of countries were able to do, however, was to present trade liberalization as part of a package that was presumed to yield large gains to the country as a whole. That is, it was not presented as, "Let's open up imports in these twenty industries, and there will be efficiency gains"; that kind of argument does not work very well in ordinary times. Instead it was, "We have to follow the strategy that everyone serious knows works: free markets including free trade—and sound money, leading to rapid economic growth."

Calling a set of economic measures a package does not mean that they need in fact be undertaken together. One can bring inflation down without liberalizing trade, and vice versa. But voters do not usually engage in hypothetical line-item vetoes, asking which elements of an economic program are essential and which can be dropped. If a program of economic stabilization-cum-liberalization seems to work, the political process is easily persuaded that all of the package is essential.

And the point was that such packages did work, and in fact initially did so astonishingly well—but not necessarily because of their fundamental economic merits. Rather, the immediate payoff to Washington consensus reforms was in the sudden improvement in investor confidence.

Mexico is particularly noteworthy. Mexico began a major program of trade liberalization in the late 1980s, with no obvious immediate results in terms of faster economic growth. The turning point came when the country negotiated a debt reduction package, which went into effect in 1990. The debt reduction was intelligently handled, but everyone involved realized that it was fairly small, not nearly enough to make much direct difference to Mexico's growth prospects.

And yet what followed the debt reduction was a transformation of the economic picture. With stunning speed, Mexico's problems seemed to melt away. Real interest rates were 30 to 40 percent before the debt deal, with the payments on internal debt a major source of fiscal pressure; they fell between 5 and 10 percent almost immediately. Mexico had been shut out of international financial markets since 1982; soon after the debt deal, capital inflows resumed on an ever-growing scale. And growth resumed in the long-stagnant economy.

Why did a seemingly modest debt reduction spark such a major change in the economic environment? International investors saw the debt deal as part of a package of reforms that they believed would work. Debt reduction went along with free markets and sound money, free markets and sound money mean prosperity, and so capital flowed into a country that was following the right path.

In the 1990s, advocates of the Washington consensus have not had to make abstruse arguments about the benefits of better resource allocation nor plead with the public to accept short-term pain in the interest of long-run gain. Instead, because the financial markets offered an immediate, generous advance on the presumed payoff from free trade and sound money, it was easy to make a case for doing the right thing and brush aside all the usual political objections.

So much for one side of the political-economic cycle. The other side involved the willingness of financial markets to provide lavish rewards for economic reform. In part, of course, the markets believed that such policies would pay off in the long run. But most of the developing countries that suddenly became investor favorites in the 1990s had long histories of disappointed expectations, not just the debt crisis of the 1980s, but track records of abandoned economic reforms reaching back for decades. Why should investors have been so confident that this time the reforms would really stick? Presumably, this time reforms were taking place so extensively, and in so many countries, that investors found it easy to believe that it was a completely new world, that runaway inflation, populist economic policies, exchange controls, and so on were vanishing from the global scene.

But I have just argued, following Rodrik, that the unprecedented depth and breadth of policy reform was largely due to the perception that such reforms brought macroeconomic and financial recovery a perception driven by the way that financial markets rewarded the reforms! So once again something of a circular logic was at work.

During the first half of the 1990s, a set of mutually reinforcing beliefs and expectations created a mood of euphoria about the prospects for the developing world. Markets poured money into developing countries, encouraged both by the capital gains they had already seen and by the belief that a wave of reform was unstoppable. Governments engaged in unprecedented liberalization, encouraged both by the self-reinforcing conventional wisdom and the undeniable fact that reformers received instant gratification from enthusiastic investors. It was a very happy picture. Why couldn't it continue?

The Reality Check

From a mere trickle during the 1980s, private capital flows to developing countries soared to about $130 billion in 1993. Relatively little of this money went to those East Asian countries that had already achieved rapid economic growth during the 1980s. Less than 10 percent of the total, for example, went to China, and the four Asian tigers—Singapore, Hong Kong, South Korea, and Taiwan—were all net exporters of capital. Instead, the bulk of the money went to countries that had done poorly in previous years, but whose new commitment to Washington consensus policies was believed to ensure a dramatic turn-around: Latin American countries, plus a few others such as the Philippines and Hungary: How well were these economies doing?

In one respect, the performance of the main recipients of massive capital inflows did represent a break with the past. The new insistence on sound money had, indeed, led to impressive reductions in inflation rates. Between 1987 and 1991, Mexico's inflation rate had averaged 49 percent; in 1994, it was less than 7 percent. In Argentina the contrast was even more spectacular, from an average inflation rate of 609 percent in 1987–91 to a rate of less than 4 percent . . . .

That was the good news. Unfortunately, there was also a substantial amount of disappointing news, on three main fronts. First, while hard currency policies brought down inflation, they did so only gradually. As a result, costs and prices got far out of line with those in the rest of the world. Mexico, for example, allowed the peso to fall only 13 percent between 1990 and the first quarter of 1994, but consumer prices in Mexico nonetheless rose 63 percent over that period, compared with a rise of only 12 percent in the United States. Thus Mexico's real exchange rate—the ratio of Mexican prices in dollars to prices in the United States—rose 28 percent, pricing many Mexican goods out of U.S. markets and fueling an import boom. Argentina's drastic policy, which sought to end a history of extreme inflation by pegging the value of the peso permanently at one dollar, predictably left the country's prices even farther out of line. Between 1990 and early 1991 the Argentine real exchange rate rose 68 percent.

Second, in spite of huge inflows of foreign capital, the real growth in the recipient economies was generally disappointing. Mexico was the biggest disappointment: although capital flows into Mexico reached more than $30 billion in 1993, the country's rate of growth over the 1990–94 period averaged only 2.5 percent, less than population growth. Other countries did better: Argentina, for example, grew at an annual average rate of more than 6 percent after the stabilization of the peso. But even optimists admitted that this growth had much to do with the extremely depressed state of the economy before the reforms. When an economy has been as thoroughly mismanaged as Argentina's was during the 1980s, a return to political and monetary stability can easily produce a large one-shot rise in output. Across Latin America as a whole, real growth in the period 1990–94 averaged only 3.1 percent per year.

Finally, the benefits of growth, which was in any case barely positive in per capita terms, were also very unevenly distributed. Developing country statistics on both unemployment and income distribution are fairly unreliable, but there is not much question that even as Latin American stock markets were booming, unemployment was rising, and the poor were getting poorer.

In sum, the real economic performance of countries that had recently adopted Washington consensus policies, as opposed to the financial returns they were delivering to international investors or the reception their policies received on the conference circuit, was distinctly disappointing. Whatever the conventional wisdom might have said, the underlying basis for the conviction of both investors and governments that these countries were on the right track was becoming increasingly fragile.

Some kind of crisis of confidence was thus inevitable. It could have come in several different ways. For example, there might have been a purely financial crisis: a loss of confidence in emerging markets as investments, leading to capital flight and only then to a loss of political confidence. Or there could have been an essentially intellectual crisis: the growing evidence that the new policies were not delivering in the way or at the speed that conventional wisdom had expected might have led to soul-searching among the policy elite. But given the way that the Washington consensus had originally come to flourish, it should not be surprising that the crisis, when it came, involved the interaction of economics and politics.

Consider the essentials of the Mexican situation as it began to unravel in 1994—the factors that would surely have provoked a crisis even without the uprisings and assassinations. Despite the popularity of the country among foreign investors, growth had slowed in 1993 to a virtual crawl, creating a considerable rise in unemployment. This growth slowdown was in a direct sense due to the rise in Mexico's real exchange rate after 1990, which discouraged any rapid growth in exports and caused growing demand to be spent primarily on imports rather than domestic goods. More fundamentally, the free market policies had not, at least so far, generated the kind of explosion of productivity, new industries, and exports that reformers hoped for.

Given these economic realities, the Mexican government was faced with a dilemma. If it wanted to get even modest growth going again, it would need to do something to make its industries more cost-competitive—that is, devalue the peso. But to do so, given the emphasis that the government had placed on sound money, would be very damaging to its credibility. In the event, the approach of the presidential election seems to have led the Mexicans neither to devalue nor to accept slow growth, but rather to reflate the economy by loosening up government spending. The result was a loss of credibility even worse than that which would have been produced by an early devaluation. And then the usual logic of currency crisis came into play: because investors thought, with some reason, that the currency might be devalued, they became unwilling to hold peso assets unless offered very high interest rates; and the necessity of paying these high rates, together with the depressing effect of high rates on the economy, increased the pressure on the government to abandon the fixed exchange rate—which made investors even less willing to hold pesos, in a rapid downward spiral familiar to scores of former finance ministers around the world.

The point is that while the details could not have been predicted, something like the Mexican crisis was bound to happen. Without the Chiapas uprising or the assassination of presidential candidate Luis Donaldo Colosio, Mexico might not have hit the wall in December 1994, but it probably would not have gone unscathed through 1995. An early, controlled devaluation might have done less damage than the display of confusion that actually took place, but it would still have done considerable harm to the government's credibility. And even if Mexico had somehow avoided getting into trouble, the disparity between the glittering prizes promised by the Washington consensus and the fairly dreary reality was bound to produce a revolution of falling expectations somewhere along the line.

An Age of Deflated Expectations?

Because the 1990–95 euphoria about developing countries was so overdrawn, the Mexican crisis is likely to be the trigger that sets the process in reverse. That is, the rest of the decade will probably be a downward cycle of deflating expectations. Markets will no longer pour vast amounts of capital into countries whose leaders espouse free markets and sound money on the assumption that such policies will necessarily produce vigorous growth; they will want to see hard evidence of such growth. This new reluctance will surely be directly self-reinforcing, in that it means that the huge capital gains in emerging market equities will not continue. It will also, more or less directly, lead to a further slowing of growth in those countries, comprising much of Latin America and several outside nations, whose hesitant recovery from the 1980s was driven largely by infusions of foreign capital.

Because reforms will no longer be instantly rewarded by the capital markets, it will be far more difficult to sell such reforms politically. Thus the common assumption that free trade and free market policies will quickly spread around the world is surely wrong. Indeed, there will doubtless be some backsliding, as the perceived failure of Washington consensus policies leads to various attempts either to restore the good old days or to emulate what are perceived as alternative models. Many developing country politicians will surely claim that truly successful development efforts have been based not on free markets and sound money but on clever planning and rationed foreign exchange. At the moment, most developing country governments are still reluctant even to hint at a return to interventionist and nationalist policies because they fear that such hints will be swiftly punished by capital flight. But sooner or later some of them will rediscover the attractions of capital controls. As has happened so many times in the past, some countries will in desperation impose regulations to discourage capital flight. They will discover that while such regulations do raise the cost of doing business, that cost seems minor compared with their newfound ability to contain temporary speculative attacks without imposing punitive interest rates.

And these two trends will surely reinforce each other. As it becomes clear to the markets that reform need not always advance, they will become increasingly reluctant to offer advances on reform. As it becomes clear that such rewards are not available even to the most virtuous of reformers, the willingness to suffer economic pain to placate the markets will erode all the more.

But will the conventional wisdom represented by the Washington consensus be so easily displaced? Before the Mexican crisis, when some warned that the rhetoric about a golden age for global capitalism was excessive, the reply was often that there was no alternative. Communism is dead. The old protectionist development strategies in South Asia and Latin America were unambiguous failures. Even if Victorian virtue does not yield the easy rewards some may have expected, it is still the only plausible course of action left. And such arguments have a point. It is, in fact, probably true that free markets and sound money—if not necessarily fixed exchange rates—are the best policy for developing countries to follow.

But it seems strangely unimaginative to assume that because there are no other popular paradigms for policy currently in circulation, nobody will be able to come up with a rationale for policies that are very much at odds with the Washington consensus. Indeed, there are already audible rumblings about emulating a supposed Asian model. Developing countries should try, some people say, to be like Japan (as they imagine it) rather than America. The intellectual basis for such ideas is far weaker than that for the Washington consensus, but to suppose that bad ideas never flourish is to ignore the lessons of history.

THE THREAT OF MODERNIZATION[4]

Yale—Nations have long looked to economic modernization as their ticket to peace and prosperity. But in the new global economy the old panacea makes less and less sense. In a world where competitive firms cross borders to seek out the lowest labor costs and where technological innovation aims to eliminate workers altogether, despite a surging population looking for jobs, the standard formula of progress has lost its promise.

Take the famous case of British Steel as a starting point. Twenty years ago British Steel was a nationalized industry, one of the largest in Europe, that employed hundreds of thousands of men and women; it was also one of the least efficient and least productive steel industries in the world. It was very uncompetitive against foreign producers, even elsewhere in Europe.

[4]Article by Paul Kennedy, historian, author, and codirector of the Secretariat to the Independent Working Group on the Future of the United Nations, from *New Perspectives Quarterly* 12:31 Ja 1 '95. Copyright © 1995 by Center for the Study of Democratic Institutions. Reprinted with permission.

Today, however, the situation is different. British Steel was denationalized and is now a private company. Its once-powerful trade union has been smashed. Thirty-three out of thirty-seven smaller, less efficient plants have been closed. Massive investments have been made in the modern steel-producing equipment. As a result, British Steel is now the most efficient steel company in Europe and among the most efficient in the world. But the cost, in terms of jobs lost, has been horrendous: Almost 85 percent of the earlier workforce has now lost their job with the company. Where once four or five men were employed, only one remains. In consequence, there is large-scale structural unemployment in most of the former steel-producing regions of Britain.

Ironically, British Steel is also the leading company that is agitating against the remaining subsidies, grants, and other financial assistance that rival steel industries in Europe obtain from their governments, arguing that such subsidies only support inefficient companies and constitute unfair trade.

This is placing European governments and steel producers in a dilemma. Many of them have closed older plants and reduced jobs, but not to British Steel's levels of labor productivity. "Yes," they say, "we'll get rid of 20 percent of steel jobs, or one-third, or even one-half—but not 80 percent. We cannot afford the social cost," they argue, "the damage felt when large-scale unemployment is inflicted upon a tightly knit steel-producing community." At the same time, they know that their subsidies are against European Community rules, and against GATT, and must be amended. But they also must admit that if they take away that financial aid, their steel producers will not be able to operate.

A second example. Until a few years ago, one of the most secure white-collar office jobs was that of settling insurance claims for the many large insurance companies situated in Hartford, CT—Prudential, the Travelers, or Aetna. Because of the rise in labor costs—not just in wages but also in such items as health-care benefits—these companies have had to find alternative, cheaper ways of dealing with insurance claims. As a consequence, now most of the standard paperwork in this service industry is no longer done in Connecticut, but in Ireland or India or Malaysia instead.

The workers in those places are fluent in English but enjoy only one-fifth or one-twentieth of the earnings of an American insurance clerk—or at least of an American clerk who is still employed, since one of the most noticeable trends in the United States economy of the last few years has been the enormous "shake-out" of jobs in industries like banking and insurance.

Even so, the relocation of the routine settling of claims from Connecticut to India is probably only an interim measure, for that process may in the future be done automatically, by machines. The same thing is true of the Japanese electrical-goods industry which has relocated assembly and production to low-labor-cost areas in Southeast Asia. Relocation is also only an interim, cost-saving measure before the full-scale automation of the process, using robotized factories with machines that receive no wages, health care or pensions.

What I have described here is a process very familiar to economists and economic historians: It is the process of modernization, whereby new and more efficient ways of making things and assembling things and servicing things replace traditional methods and practices.

Steam power replaces human and animal muscle; the automobile replaces the horse; electricity replaces candlelight. The result is bad news for handloom-weavers, and for blacksmiths and coachmen, not to mention candlestick-makers; but it is beneficial in a macroeconomic sense. For, not only does it increase labor productivity and standards of living, but the newer jobs—those associated with steam engines and automobiles and the electrical industry—both require and create a better-trained, better-educated workforce.

Was not this process to be seen, in its classical form, in the metamorphosis of the U.S. economy over the past two hundred years? In the early decades of the American Republic, over nine-tenths of the populace was engaged in agriculture and related activities. Slowly, and then with quickening pace, people moved from the agricultural sector to the industrial sector.

As American society became more wealthy, it also became more complex—banks, restaurants, shops, gas stations, schools, leisure activities, all grew fast, and people began moving out of the manufacturing sector into the services sector. Agriculture continued to shrink in the numbers it employed, though steadily increasing its rate of labor productivity. Greater foreign competition in low-cost, low-level manufacturing, then later on in medium-to-upper-level manufacturing, intensified the process. At present the U.S. may have only 3 to 4 percent of its population in the agricultural sector, perhaps about 18 percent in industry, and 70 to 75 percent in services. Is this not, then, a natural process, due to be followed by all other societies?

Perhaps it is, but a glance at today's global economic condition, with all its complexities and contradictions, suggests that we should not automatically assume that this form of relatively benign modernization will spread from continent to continent—or even that the process of late has been benign, as my examples of British Steel and Connecticut insurance companies seem to contradict. There is a need, rather, to ask a few large and searching questions.

From what new inventions, and in what new fields, might we expect future job-multiplying industries? The shipbuilding industry of Western Europe in the 17th and 18th centuries was one such multiplier, stimulating many ancillary trades and industries. The steam-driven textile machines were another multiplier; the mid-19th-century railway was another; the automobile was an even greater job-multiplier. In more recent times we might list the aircraft industry and air transportation. They were job-multipliers because, say, the automobile generated not just employment in Ford or Hyundai factories, but among thousands of suppliers, gas-station attendants and highway-construction crews.

In addition, the per capita "added value" of these new inventions was higher than that of the products they replaced. An automobile worker thus earned more than a blacksmith. Today's new technologies, like biotech, however, seem to require only Ph.D.s —or, like robotics, to be destroying more jobs than they create.

When I ask my economist friends to name an emerging job-multiplying industry that will raise wages (unlike jobs in the fast-food industry) they are silent—or point perhaps to health care. Is looking after the sick the only significant job-multiplying trend of the early 21st century?

What if no new industries are arising in regions where traditional occupations are being made redundant—as, say, in northern or western parts of France? Agriculture's share of employment continues to tumble, despite vast subsidies; steel, coal, and metal-making shrinks and shrinks. Even Euro-Disney doesn't work. Where is new work?

A related question: How do we best pay the "social costs" of shedding, as in the case of British Steel, 80 percent of jobs in an inefficient industry? Do we invite people to move elsewhere, in the American manner? Do we pay them unemployment insurance, as in the British and French method? Do we invest in retraining and retooling skills, as in Scandinavia? What will the political repercussions be? A right-wing backlash? Protectionism against foreign goods?

Granted that we cannot halt modernization, and that it has provided a long-term stimulus to global economic growth over the past 250 years, how do economists, businessmen or politicians handle processes like the automation of the factory and the office that reduce more jobs than they create? A new invention is one thing; a new invention specifically designed to get human beings out of the workplace is another.

Granted, again, that modernization is unstoppable, how does it work when production of an item takes place not just in a specific region like Western Europe in the 19th century or East Asia in the late 20th century, but globally when there are fifty countries, with varying standards of wages, capable of producing soybeans, and seventy countries capable of producing steel?

Adam Smith's famous argument in favor of free trade and specialization (that it made no economic sense for both England and Portugal to strive to produce wine and textiles when England's climate made it a better textile producer and Portugal's climate made it a better wine producer) doesn't address this reality of multiple competitive sources. Yet, that is the basis of modern, free-market economics. What if there is nothing you can produce more cheaply or efficiently than anywhere, except by constantly cutting labor costs?

Many of these questions were asked by previous societies undergoing change, but today's pressures may be the more intense because the transformations are much faster and they affect billions of people. If China, Mexico, and Brazil are expected to undergo, in the space of one to two generations, the modernization process that evolved over a century and a half in Britain and America, should we really be surprised that their social fabric is under stress?

What would the world look like if, sometime next century, it replicated the U.S. in the percentages of the population engaged in each economic sector—if, globally, only 3 to 6 percent ended up in agriculture, rather than the 50–80 percent in many developing countries today? Where would all those farmers and peasants have gone to? The cities? The insurance companies? The health-care services?

Can we imagine a world of 8.5–10 billion people, the vast majority of whom are engaged in services? Would there also be intense competition in this field as, say, lower-paid lawyers in India offered their services to customers in America or Germany or Australia? Just how far does modernization and global competition go, before it challenges every activity, every job, every practice? Like national self-determination, laissez-faire in trade is a principle of which we generally approve. But do we want to push the principle to its ultimate logical conclusion?

Finally, and perhaps the most politically explosive question of all, what are the implications of the continuing growth in world population, especially in poorer countries desperate to find jobs for their adolescent populations?

If each year we add another 95 million people to the Earth's total, then each year we need to create an additional 40 million jobs globally. If we cannot produce decent employment for millions of young people in America, Europe, Russia, perhaps even Japan now, what prospects do we offer to the emerging hundreds of millions of men and women in the developing world?

And why should we be surprised, when we project television programs like Dallas and Brideshead Revisited to the North African littoral or the Atacama Desert, that millions of young, ambitious people are planning to move toward richer, Northern countries in the hope of getting a job?

And after all, why shouldn't they? This is an age in which virtually all of what the classical economists termed "the factors of production" are being liberated. Finance, trade, intellectual property, patents, cultural programs, tourists, exchange students—everything is becoming part of a globalized system.

But there is one factor of production that is not being allowed to roam across borders at will—labor, people, human beings. Isn't there a basic contradiction here? Isn't this precisely one of the greatest challenges that our global society faces as it doubles from five billion to ten billion people in the coming half-century?

I don't know the answers to these questions, but I do know that the questions themselves are beginning to be asked, in parts of Europe, in parts of America and in other regions of the globe. Should we try to manage trade to soften the blows of dislocation? Should the World Trade Organization set to supplant GATT and all those regional trade blocs like NAFTA that seek to liberalize commerce not also place on their agenda liberalized migration?

The momentum of global integration has placed these issues of jobs and migration front and center. Marx once said that history only presents those questions for which its own development will yield answers. Let us hope that, just this once, he was right.

BACK TO THE FUTURE[5]

The end of history looks a lot like the beginning of this century. The dominant trend in politics and economics then as now was liberalization. Regimes across the globe were moving toward freer markets and more representative governments. World trade was booming, and standards of living were moving up steadily. National economies were getting increasingly intertwined; perhaps even more so than they are today. Using a simple measure of economic interdependence—exports plus imports as a percentage of GNP—we see that late 19th-century Britain, France, Germany, and Italy ranged between 33 and 52 percent, slightly higher than comparable figures today. Borders were permeable and travel seamless. Today you do not need visas to move within Europe; then you did not even need a passport. A. L. Rowse has called that age of truly borderless commerce "the belle epoque of interdependence."

To be sure, this growth brought with it turmoil, fear, and uncertainty, as change always does. Certain nations, and certain sectors and sections within nations, did better than others. On the whole, however, it was a time of progress on several fronts. Between 1870 and 1900 world industrial production quadrupled. Every day a new invention or advance in health or technology would dazzle the world. Even so gloomy a writer as Emile Zola hailed "a century of science and democracy."

[5]Article by Fareed Zakaria, managing editor of *Foreign Affairs*, from *National Review* 47:54+ D 11 '95. Copyright © 1995 by National Review Inc. Reprinted with permission.

It was possible to look at this world at the dawn of the century and assume it would continue forever. As John Maynard Keynes wrote, most observers "regarded this state of affairs as normal, certain, and permanent, except in the direction of further improvement, and any deviation from it as aberrant, scandalous, and avoidable." The British liberal intellectual Norman Angell explained that Europe's economies had become so dependent on each other, technology so powerful, and stability so important to everyone, that war among the advanced nations was unthinkable, impossible, and obsolete. His book, *The Great Illusion*, was published in 1913.

World War I is commonly believed to have brought this world tumbling down. It did not. The decline of British power, hastened to be sure by the war, was the larger cause. The system of liberal economics and politics rested on the massive edifice of British power. Britain played the role of balancer in Europe, producing a century of political stability, and its immense navy spread that stability beyond the continent. By practicing unilateral free trade, with the repeal of the Corn Laws in 1846, Britain created the first (relatively) open world economy. The City of London, the Bank of England, the pound, and the gold standard provided the financial stability that allowed international transactions to flow freely and capital to move where it was most needed. The collapse of British power by the 1920s, and the refusal of the United States to take Britain's place, unhinged this global economic system. Depression, mercantilism, xenophobia, and war followed almost inevitably.

The world we are living in now, with an open economy, free trade, liberalizing regimes, and increasingly borderless travel, is also undergirded by political stability and power—American power. The centerpiece of this world is the Organization for Economic Co-operation and Development, made up of countries that were once warring enemies and are now trading friends. They have produced the greatest economic miracle in human history—one that makes even the Marxist historian E. J. Hobsbawm term 1945–89 "the golden age of capitalism." This golden age has rested on five pillars: the political unity that resulted from the Soviet threat; America's security guarantee, which made unnecessary separate (and possibly competing) national defense policies; the free-trade system, sponsored by the United States; the dollar's pivotal role in the international monetary system; and American public and private investment abroad.

This world is under some strain. The Soviet threat provided a glue that held these rivals together; that glue is fast thinning. In the cultural, political, and military realm, American power is utterly preeminent in the world. But American economic power, though still unrivaled, has been eroding for twenty-five years from forces largely beyond the government's control—the rise of newly industrializing countries, the pace of technological change, etc. But some American policies have hurt. For most of its modern (post-Civil War) history the United States was a high-savings-and-investment economy. By the 1960s it was consuming more and investing less, and the massive Keynesian state spending of that era, coupled with the Vietnam War, accelerated this trend. By the 1970s American productivity rates, once the envy of the world at 3 percent, were down to 0.8 percent. Today America leads the world in consumption and lags it in investment.

This shift in power has had economic effects. The world monetary system came apart in 1973 and is now patched together by ad hoc arrangements and summit meetings. The global free-trade system is in danger of being subverted by regional blocs like the European Community, bilateralism among the newly industrializing countries of East Asia, and rising protectionism in every major industrial country, including the United States.

Rather than sketch what the world will look like in the future, let me suggest what it could look like if the United States pursued a policy consciously designed to sustain and widen the post-1945 world that it created.

First, the United States would put its fiscal house in order. Structural budget deficits that arise from ever-increasing entitlement spending would be narrowed and eliminated. Perhaps there would even be a surplus some years! The federal government would become more effective at its core functions while shedding the accumulated baggage of tasks it has taken over from local governments, the private sector, and civil society over the last thirty years. American tax policies would be altered to reward once again savings and investment and restrain consumption. Productivity rates would start rising again.

These structural shifts in the American economy would inevitably affect the trade deficit with Japan, easing pressure for foolish protectionist policies toward the second largest economy in the world. The shifts would also inevitably have a favorable effect on the value of the dollar and strengthen its role as the world's reserve currency.

The United States would invite Germany and Japan—as the two other economic superpowers—to join with it and take ambitious steps to halt the deterioration of the open world economic system. It would invite them to help strengthen those international economic rules, regimes, and institutions that are fraying. They would totally restructure organizations like the International Monetary Fund and the World Bank that need new missions in a new world, and junk those that were obsolete.

Peace can be kept only by power and not by international law or some mechanistic system like collective security. America would maintain the world's largest armed forces and maintain its security guarantees to Western Europe and Japan and Korea. It would try to organize a loose concert of great powers. This system would make the same assumptions the 19th-century concert of Europe did—that while each great power has its own, distinct interests, they all want to avoid a general war. America would particularly try to integrate the two outsiders, Russia and China, into the international system. But were either power to make bids for hegemony in the vital areas of the world they inhabit, the United States would help neighboring countries to deter or contain this threat to international stability.

The newly industrializing nations of East Asia and Latin America would increasingly integrate themselves into the world economy and the international community. Not every country's economy would grow, but many would, and the resulting global prosperity would provide the funds to tackle some transnational problems like environmental degradation. The post-1945 world has had many problems, but on the whole it is one that has resulted in extraordinary progress toward peace, democracy, material well-being, and civilized conduct.

This is an optimistic but not utopian view of the future. Poverty, disease, conflict, and war would all persist, but this system would prevent the two largest tragedies that could afflict the world: a great-power war and a massive disruption in the global economic system. Putting it this way might make it sound less ambitious than it is. But peace among the great powers is rare in history. A functioning world economy is rarer still. The United States built this uncommon world. It is the best one we've known. It would be a tragedy if it were to founder because the United States lost faith in its own handiwork.

II. NAFTA'S RESULTS

Editor's Introduction

The North American Free Trade Agreement has traveled an arduous road, and even some free-traders have voiced opposition to it. This section analyzes the various points of view about NAFTA. The first article, by Rick Henderson, reprinted from *Reason*, explores NAFTA's potential and argues that to reduce the number of "deal makers and shakedown artists," free-traders should try to identify and resolve the problems with these trade agreements themselves. In support of his argument, Henderson compares the commercial trade policies of Japan with those of the United States, citing a controversy between Fuji and Kodak.

Mark Potok, writing for *USA Today*, looks at new provisions of NAFTA that may squeeze Mexicans out of jobs. These new regulations weaken competition between Mexican and American truck drivers, since most Mexican drivers fail U.S. safety standards. Broadly speaking, President Clinton's promise that NAFTA would create jobs on both sides of the border has fallen short. And with travel restrictions along the border eased, drug trafficking is likely to increase.

Elaborating on NAFTA's effects on drug trafficking is "Narco-Power and the Subterranean NAFTA," by Eduardo Valle. This article discusses the surprising power of the drug trade in Mexico. New NAFTA provisions that pose a threat to the drug cartels have provoked terrorists to assassinate two prominent Mexican leaders. Within Mexico, drug money has penetrated banking, tourism, construction, transportation, and agriculture. President Ernesto Zedillo of Mexico has vowed to bring the criminals and their associates to justice.

"NAFTA's First Real Test," reprinted from *Audubon*, investigates the death of migratory birds in the Silva reservoir, where high concentrations of metal are believed to have killed an estimated 40,000 migratory birds during the winter of 1994. The contamination could also lead to human deaths. Author Talli Nauman suggests that NAFTA's loose enforcement of protection codes has contributed to this ecological disaster.

Ramesh Ponnuru's article, reprinted from *National Review*, focuses on Patrick Buchanan as the first presidential candidate of the election year to challenge free trade. Free-traders like Ponnuru believes that Buchanan's views of protectionism are his "way to signal his solidarity with working class Americans" for a short-term political advantage; Ponnuru argues that in the long run protectionism will operate to the disadvantage of American workers.

Lastly, "Grading Free Trade," reprinted from *The Nation*, gives a report on the performance of NAFTA to date. David Corn states that growth of free trade has been "disappointing" and that the United States and Mexico have been unable to enforce the agreement's provisions. With NAFTA's failings difficult to resolve under the present guidelines, the original agreement may have to be amended, at the cost of renewed controversy at home and abroad.

UNRULY OPTIONS[1]

Why Arguments For Unilateral Free Trade Don't Work

. . . Before the Clinton administration declared victory in the auto wars, U.S. Trade Representative Mickey Kantor had already opened another front in the perpetual campaign against Japan: the battle between film makers Kodak and Fuji. Kodak says Fuji and the Japanese government have colluded to keep Kodak out of the Japanese market—closing off access to wholesale distributors, offering discounts to retailers that offer only Fuji film, buying up film-processing facilities. *BusinessWeek* called Kodak's case against Fuji "promising." "Kodak has a much clearer case than the U.S. automakers did," said *Time*. "Many trade pros think Kodak's case is far stronger," agreed *Newsweek*.

Fuji has countered with a credible case that, here in the United States, Kodak engages in many of the same "noncompetitive"

[1]Article by Rick Henderson, from the October 1995 issue of REASON Magazine 27:7. Copyright © 1995 by the Reason Foundation. Reprinted with permission.

practices it accuses Fuji of perpetrating in Japan. And as one attorney representing Fuji told me, "This is a classic example of two huge companies beating the shit out of each other in markets all over the world—to the benefit of consumers."

The attorney's argument is absolutely correct. And it has no chance of prevailing in the current political environment. The debate, after all, pits a corporation based in notoriously protectionist Japan against one headquartered in the more-or-less free-trading United States. With such visible players haggling over access to a common consumer product, the big picture—micromanaging film sales would hurt consumers—can become obscured.

That's why free traders might want to reconsider the argument . . . that the United States should bypass such multilateral pacts as the North American Free Trade Agreement and the General Agreement on Tariffs and Trade and set trade policy unilaterally. After all, the Clinton administration is in fact bypassing GATT now and the results haven't enhanced free trade. Negotiating ponderous, flawed treaties may not be the best way to open markets, but right now, it's the only game in town.

Since the days of Adam Smith, free traders have argued that an unimpeded flow of goods and services benefits the individual consumer because competitive pressures will force entrepreneurs to offer the best products at the lowest possible price. These "classical" arguments remain true. But in today's political marketplace, they aren't enough. Understanding trade policy requires a different economic calculus: public choice.

Public-choice pioneers James Buchanan and Gordon Tullock explained that when the people who benefit from a public policy are visible and organized—say, the stockholders and employees of Kodak—and those harmed by the policy are dispersed and disorganized—millions of film buyers—concentrated political interests will tend to trump the public good. Mickey Kantor's tenure as trade representative exemplifies this approach.

In a June 25, 1995 *Washington Times* op-ed, Kantor spelled out his goals for U.S.-Japan trade policy: "creating a balanced trade relationship with Japan." Kantor touted the "fourteen market-opening agreements we have concluded with Japan in areas including telecommunications, flat glass, insurance, and medical technology." Kantor, who has called these agreements

"WTO-plus," writes, "The stubborn refusal of Japanese negotia-tors to open their markets is the crux of the problem—not ab-stract concerns about free trade, or U.S. 'bullying,' or the intricacies of international trade rules." Kantor suggests that he plans to negotiate more narrowly targeted agreements, no doubt preceded by plenty of bluster and acrimony.

Unilateralists in both parties want to formulate trade policy, but the Republicans appear no more interested in reducing barri-ers than their Democratic counterparts. With remarkable insensi-tivity to car buyers and dealers, Newt Gingrich has suggested treating the stubborn Japanese as the French would: Require ev-ery Japanese car entering the United States to be inspected at a single port, say, Seattle, manned by only seven inspectors, half of whom are on vacation at any given time. Presidential front-runner Bob Dole is a legendary deal maker whose long-standing closeness to Dwayne Andreas, CEO of agribusiness giant Archer Daniels Midland, isn't encouraging. And if the populist right con-tinues to demand concessions from Dole before giving him its support, what might Pat Buchanan, whose campaign is under-written by arch-protectionist textile magnate Roger Milliken, de-mand?

"Rules-based" trade deals like GATT and NAFTA are rid-dled with loopholes, take years to complete, and require armies of lawyers and bureaucrats to implement. But these pacts attempt to limit rogue actors like Kantor and Gingrich. They allow devel-oping nations—who want to sell to world markets—to act as sur-rogates for the diffuse interests of American consumers. And the completion of one agreement establishes momentum for wider negotiations that can help more barriers fall.

Multilateral treaties may not offer the ideal path to free trade. But at least they reduce the influence of deal makers and shake-down artists.

NAFTA RULE USHERS IN UNSAFE TRUCKS[2]

Some politicians and union leaders fear a wave of unsafe trucks from Mexico, many carrying hazardous materials, as a key provision of the North American Free Trade Agreement [took] effect [on December 18, 1995].

But travel restrictions won't automatically be lifted . . . for Mexican trucks carrying goods to and from border states, says Steven Akey, spokesman for Secretary of Transportation Federico Pena.

Mexican trucking companies must apply to the Interstate Commerce Commission (ICC) for a registration certificate and meet certain standards.

"The ICC will have forty-five days to rule on those applications, so traffic doesn't increase today," Akey said . . . .

Some congressional leaders, state officials, and the Teamsters union say Mexican trucks routinely carry toxic waste, jet fuels, and pesticides, yet fail U.S. safety standards.

They also argue that drivers work too many hours and often are inexperienced and uninsured. They have been pressuring President Clinton to delay opening the border.

Another concern is that unrestricted travel will cause an increase in drug trafficking from Mexico.

Leon Flores Gonzales, vice president of Mexico's Chamber of Transport, says the accusations are "insulting lies."

"Those Americans think we still ride donkeys," he told the Monterrey, Mexico-based newspaper *El Norte*.

But there also has been pressure on Mexican officials to delay the . . . deadline. Mexican drivers, already hit by their country's financial crisis, fear competition from U.S. drivers will push them out of jobs.

"They are coming to take food from our tables," says Sabino Cruz Munoz, 58, who has been transporting coffee, vegetables, and fruits from tropical Veracruz state for the past forty years. "We don't want the free trade agreement."

[2]Article by Mark Potok, from *USA Today* D 18 '95. Copyright © 1995. USA TODAY. Reprinted with permission.

NAFTA lifted trade restrictions between the USA, Canada, and Mexico. Canadian trucks already have access to U.S. roads, and U.S. truckers can drive through Canada.

Now, Mexican trucks will be able to travel throughout Texas, New Mexico, Arizona, and California. They had been limited to a 17-mile strip along the border to drop cargo.

The issue has become a political problem for Clinton, who pushed NAFTA and said it would create jobs. Two states Clinton needs to carry to get re-elected—Texas and California—want to delay opening the border until it's clear Mexican trucks meet standards.

"There are bald tires, faulty brakes, faulty steering systems, mechanical problems, and concerns about driver training," says Texas Attorney General Dan Morales. "Heaven forbid if it were to take a fatal accident to get the attention of federal officials."

The Arizona legislature tightened regulation of Mexican vehicles . . . . Still, officials there don't think the effects will be that bad since many trucks don't drive into the interior part of the state.

More than 80 percent of Mexican-American trade passes through Texas, 75 percent of it by truck.

Morales has asked federal officials to allow Texas inspectors to enter customs yards to check trucks for safety.

Just 150 of the 5,000 trucks that cross into Texas daily are inspected. Texas plans to add 109 inspectors, but they'll still inspect only a small fraction of trucks. By the year 2000 it's estimated that cross-border truck volume could quadruple.

In one recent period, inspectors at Laredo turned back 530 of 744 Mexican trucks for safety violations. Nearly half exceeded weight limits. Morales says a quarter of Mexican trucks carry potentially deadly hazardous materials.

Frank Vida, past president of the Laredo Transportation Association, says Mexican drivers generally are very good. He says Mexican firms recently have upgraded their trucks.

Regulations for Truckers

For Mexican truck drivers entering the USA:
• Registration certificate from Interstate Commerce Commission. Application fee, $300; can take forty-five days.

- Liability insurance.
- Proper driver's license.
- Vehicle licensing and registration.
- Oversize/overweight permits, if applicable.
- For trucks carrying hazardous materials, license from state, shipping papers in English, exterior signs listing truck contents.
- Vehicles may be inspected by U.S. Customs or state officials.

For U.S. truck drivers entering Mexico:
- Immigration papers issued by Mexican consulate.
- Import permit and vehicle permit issued by Department of Commerce and Industrial Development.
- Authorization from Department of Communications and Transport.
- Liability insurance.
- Proper driver's license.

NARCO-POWER AND
THE SUBTERRANEAN NAFTA[3]

Washington—The assassinations . . . [in 1994] of Luis Donaldo Colosio, the candidate of the ruling Institutional Revolutionary Party (PRI) designated by then-President Carlos Salinas to succeed him in office, and Jose Francisco Ruiz Massieu, the Secretary General of the PRI, have exposed an alarming reality: Narco-power is becoming a state within a state in Mexico.

In his last state-of-the-nation address on November 3, [1994] President Salinas himself was obliged to acknowledge for the first time publicly that drug trafficking "is intertwined with the violence we have suffered in Mexico" over the past year.

Alongside the North American Free Trade (NAFTA) zone painstakingly negotiated by officials from the United States, Canada, and Mexico is another reality—the underground free-trade zone for narcotics patched together by cruel bands of criminals

[3]Article by Eduardo Valle, from *New Perspectives Quarterly* 12:60 Ja 1 '95. Copyright © 1995 by Center for the Study of Democratic Institutions. Reprinted with permission.

whose network stretches from the Mexican border to Arizona and Texas, from California to New York, from Miami to Chicago.

This subterranean trade is dominated by the powerful multinational Gulf Cartel believed to be led by Juan Garcia Abrego and linked to the Ciudad Juarez Cartel. They corrupt everything in their violent and cash-rich reach, including politics.

Unless their growing power is contained, it will spread to challenge the security of the rule of law in an increasingly integrated North America. In the past two decades, since the "gomeros," as the drug traffickers are known, began pushing cocaine northward for the Colombian Cali Cartel, they have become "the other power" in Mexico.

In 1994, with the NAFTA treaty in place, and as the most vigorously contested presidential race in modern Mexican history was conducted, the party of narco-power launched an armed insurrection against the rule of law. Through the terror of assassination, they have intimidated the Mexican political class that is trying to make Mexico a partner in legitimate commerce and democracy with the U.S. The drug cartels fully understand that the greatest threat to their subterranean commerce is the non-tariff barrier of the law.

First, Mexico was the location for the production of marijuana, opium, and black heroin. Later, the country became the main transit point for cocaine from Colombia. With the enormously lucrative growth of the cocaine trade, the demand for which grew geometrically in U.S. cities over the past two decades, came the need for greater political protection of the business.

Too much was at stake for the petty payoffs that had ensured an official here or there would look the other way. That greater protection was provided by elements within the federal state and also by the "caciques," or political bosses, at the local and state level. In short, the political authoritarianism of the Mexican presidential system and the weakness of democratic institutions created and fed its own Frankenstein.

Initially, in the 1970s, the old guard of the PRI accommodated the narco-traffickers for the obvious reason: The flow of dollars that surged from contraband trade was too attractive to ignore. The enriching payoffs were large and entailed no direct consequence to public order. But, by the end of Jose Lopez Portillo's presidency in the 1980s, money from narco-trafficking needed to be invested because the assets had grown so large. In this way, drug funds penetrated the whole system: banks, tourism, construction, aviation and other transportation, and agriculture.

No one knows the exact amount of the assets involved. But it is said that the Mexican cartels today take as much as 40 percent of the street price of Colombian cocaine as the fee for their mediating role in getting it into U.S. markets.

According to the authoritative newsletter *Mexico Report*, the profits from drugs moving through Mexico into the U.S. every year are more than twice the total revenues of Mexico's petroleum industry, and will roughly equal the cost of servicing Mexico's $160 billion foreign debt for 1994.

By the time Miguel de la Madrid took office, after Lopez Portillo, he found two crises confronting Mexico: Economic collapse due to falling oil prices and the hidden crisis of narco-power with which he had to directly contend in order to govern. This was a crisis known only to the party heads and by the group closest to the president known as "The Happy Family."

In their way, Mexican officials up until [now] . . . have made their pact with narco-power, either by directly protecting the traffickers or implicitly by not pressing the challenge against their political allies, which would disrupt the shaky balance of power in the ruling PRI. It is this balance that is unraveling today in the aftermath of the assassination of Ruiz Massieu, as the trail of blood apparently leads from the Gulf Cartel ever higher and higher into the ranks of the PRI.

Mexicans do not yet know if Ernesto Zedillo, Mexico's new president, will accommodate the pressures of the traffickers and negotiate with their political representatives, or if he will seek a long-range strategy with Canada and the U.S. to subdue the narco-power that increasingly challenges the rule of law.

For now, Zedillo has declared in Matamoros, birthplace of the Gulf Cartel, that drug traffickers "and those associated with them" will be fought with all the state's power. And he has appointed a member of the opposition PAN party as his attorney general. If Zedillo sticks to this course, there may be hope yet for escaping the criminal undertow of narco-power that could turn Mexico into another Colombia.

The eruption of long-dormant violence in Mexico's political life . . . can be the writing on the wall of worse to come. Or it can provide the opportunity to raise to the highest priority Mexico's most pressing challenge in the NAFTA era: Establishing the rule of law across the land.

NAFTA'S FIRST REAL TEST[4]

Environmentalists force an investigation into the deaths of migratory birds in Mexico. As they do annually, thousands of birds migrating south from Canada and the United States stopped [during the] winter [of 1994] at central Mexico's Silva Reservoir to rest and feed. Unlike in other years, though, an estimated 40,000 died there—victims of the reservoir's contaminated water.

Throughout December and January [1995], twenty-one birds—including ruddy ducks, northern pintails, green-winged teals, and white-faced ibises—were killed at Silva, poisoned by the polluted reservoir. The deaths drew international attention, and on June 7 the National Audubon Society requested the first investigation under the environmental side accord of the . . . North American Free Trade Agreement (NAFTA).

The reservoir, located in Guanajuato State, has been drained and the corpses buried; but with just months to go before scores of migratory birds return to the area, environmentalists are anxious to see the results of the NAFTA investigation. Two Mexican conservation organizations, the Group of 100 and the Mexican Center for Environmental Law, joined Audubon in filing its petition with the North American Commission for Environmental Cooperation, which was created under NAFTA to monitor environmental problems in the three member countries.

Although the commission—funded by Canada, the United States, and Mexico—has no punitive powers, it is investigating the cause of the deaths and the Mexican government's response. Audubon officials expect the commission to release its preliminary report in October [1995]. The petition, filed at the agency's headquarters in Montreal, also asks the commission to seek technical assistance and international funding from sources such as the World Bank for cleaning up the Silva watershed.

[4]Article by Talli Nauman, from *Audubon* S/O '95. Copyright © 1995 by *Audubon*. Reprinted with permission.

The Mexican government initially attributed the bird deaths at Silva to the pesticide endosulfan. However, the results of subsequent water tests showed high concentrations of chromium, lead, arsenic, and other heavy metals used by an intensive leather-tanning and shoe industry just upstream in the city of León, which has no industrial-waste-treatment facility. Despite the test results, the tanneries in León, which is known as the shoemaking capital of Mexico, deny responsibility for the pollution—as do local agrochemical companies.

Discharge into the reservoir has been banned, but the lake-bed sediments are still contaminated by heavy metals. The reservoir will remain drained until the contamination is cleaned up. The pollution affects not only the birds but also hundreds of small farmers and ranchers in the area who depend on the reservoir for irrigation and water for their livestock.

Kathleen Rogers, lead counsel for the Audubon Society in the precedent-setting NAFTA case, notes that the exact cause of the birds' death may never be determined. But "migratory birds are a shared resource," she says. "The long-term effect on those birds that survived is unknown. . . . Lingering contaminants may pose a threat to U.S. and Canadian hunters . . . . What's important is to get on with the investigation, issue a report, and develop a plan to protect both game and nongame birds."

Local residents say that birds have been dying at the tainted reservoir for more than a decade—though never in such large numbers. However, over a two-week period in December, the number of deaths rose at such an alarming rate that local environmentalists felt compelled to take action. The Guanajuato Ecological Foundation, a group of ten scientists who discovered the carnage, organized volunteers to retrieve sick and dying birds.

Through much of [the 1994] winter . . . volunteers hauled out thousands of weak and drooping birds, reviving more than 1,000 of them with injections of antibiotics and vitamins and releasing them at nearby reservoirs. To hold the dead and decaying birds, five common graves were dug beside the Silva Reservoir; early in the rescue effort, the graves were simply left open, each day's layer of remains dusted with lime and dirt.

"It's terrible how they're mounting up," Martha Ramirez, a biologist with the Guanajuato foundation, said . . . . "We have seen so many dead . . . ."

In December [1994], the foundation registered a formal complaint with the Mexican government. Fearing that Mexican officials would fail to take action, the foundation appealed to the National Audubon Society for help. "We wanted them to support us in obtaining rules that really have force," Ramirez says. "Mexico is going through some very hard times. The environment is seriously deteriorating. Unfortunately, it is one of the issues that our government really has not taken action on."

Over the years other wildlife has also suffered at Silva according to foundation biologist Martin Rodriguez. "The frog's song was last heard at this site fifteen years ago," he says. Carp and other fish that once attracted anglers to the reservoir have long since vanished; dogs, reptiles, turtles, and entire ant populations have also died.

The effects of the polluted reservoir are not limited to the immediate area. Water from Silva runs into the Turbio River, a major tributary of the Lerma Chapala Basin. The basin, one of Mexico's largest and most important, provides 17 percent of the domestic water for Mexico City, feeds 150 lakes in five states, and eventually empties into the Pacific Ocean.

Homero Aridjis, leader of the Group of 100, says the pollution in the basin highlights a national lack of sewage treatment and control of toxic substances. At least eleven Mexican watersheds have been classified as highly contaminated by the government's water commission. "Here we're talking about the ducks," Aridjis says, "but there also are effects on human health."

NAFTA environmental commission biologists and officials, including executive director Victor Lichtinger, traveled to the reservoir on June 17, [1995]—ten days after Audubon filed its petition—to talk to local residents and get a firsthand look at the polluted site. The next day Lichtinger announced the commission's decision to undertake the first trinational investigation under the terms of the NAFTA side accord. "We're going to study the situation and draw regional attention to what might otherwise be seen as a local problem," he said.

Lichtinger then took part in a public forum with Julia Carabias, Mexico's minister of environment, natural resources, and fisheries, who welcomes the investigation, saying it will be useful for both Mexico and its North American partners. In February [1995], in response to public pressure over the reservoir, Carabias had launched a joint government, citizen, and business committee to oversee remedial efforts in the Turbio Basin. She said the price tag for cleanup measures would be nearly $87.5 million.

Mary Minette, an Audubon staff attorney in Washington, D.C., who evaluated the situation at Silva in March [1995], said, "Mexico's water-pollution protection codes are just as good as those of the United States or Canada. The Mexican authorities are just not enforcing them."

"If this focuses attention on the Silva area of Mexico and the problems of enforcement, it will bring resources into play such as technical know-how from other countries and development assistance. We're looking at this with the idea that we may be doing Mexico a service by building some international pressure."

FAIR TRADE, FOUL POLITICS[5]

Protectionists are a minority in the Republican Party—but a growing one. There are a number of reasons for this. The postwar bipartisan consensus in favor of free trade rested on beliefs about American leadership of the world which younger Republican congressmen tend not to share. Then again, as a result of the postwar decision to pursue free trade multilaterally rather than unilaterally, free trade has become linked to international entanglements of which conservatives have long and justifiably been suspicious. And that decision has had other consequences. The multilateral approach makes it seem that free trade is a good idea only if it's a two-way street (whereas the classical case for free trade asserts that trade barriers harm the nation that imposes them regardless of its trading partners' policies). Protectionist sentiment thus increases when countries are perceived, fairly or not, as closed to American exports. And, finally, there is Pat Buchanan.

Mr. Buchanan is the first Republican presidential candidate to challenge the postwar GOP orthodoxy on free trade. Because he is a conservative in good standing on cultural issues—indeed, a courageous conservative champion in what was for years the

[5]Article by Ramesh Ponnuru, from *National Review* 47:52 N 6 '95. Copyright © 1995 by National Review Inc. Reprinted with permission.

generally unsympathetic media—he has built up a stock of good-will on the Right. And contrary to his image, he is a thinker with a love of history who takes the trouble to master, hone, and argue his case in public debate. So, when he complains that "the Japanese . . . have been taking advantage of America" and labels them "predatory traders," he is heeded where others might be ignored.

He has been helped in his campaign by the reluctance of free-traders on the Right to take their case to the public. Republican presidential candidates who espouse free trade, like Phil Gramm, consider it too difficult to explain the benefits of free trade in a campaign. Other free-traders have said surprisingly little to counter Buchanan's arguments. Or, worse, they have simply sneered. James Bovard says of him, "He's going to have a certain appeal to people who have never been able to balance a checkbook and are still afraid of the dark." Comments like that make it easy for Mr. Buchanan to depict free-traders as elitists. Since free trade in fact enjoys more support from elites than from the general public, it has come under suspicion as conservatism has taken an increasingly populist cast. Pat Buchanan and his allies stirred up considerable grass-roots opposition to NAFTA and GATT by framing them as elite frauds against the public. Protectionism, in contrast, offers conservatives an easy way to signal their solidarity with working-class Americans.

These are all solid political advantages—in the short term. But the essential test of a policy is more mundane: Will it work? Because if protectionism won't work, then it won't produce popularity or sustain an administration in office. And both economic theory and experience give us a pretty good idea of exactly how protectionism won't work.

To begin with, it would raise prices for both consumer goods and capital goods. It would therefore almost certainly increase unemployment: as prices for protected goods rose, industries that use them and even some of the protected industries would shrink. Mr. Buchanan attaches far more importance to the trade deficit than it deserves—he recently described it as the "worst" of President Clinton's failures—but it is not clear that his proposals would affect it. Trade barriers would reduce both the incentive for American companies to export from the sheltered home market (by causing the exchange rate to appreciate) and their ability to do so (by raising their supply costs).

Nor would his proposed "social tariff" against the Third World protect American workers' wages to any great extent, because cheap labor has not been as important in international competition as he believes. If it were, companies would have moved in droves to Haiti and Bangladesh. They have not done so, because they look at wages in relation to productivity. American wages are higher than those in developing nations not because U.S. workers have been shielded from competition, but because they are more productive. The route to higher American wages therefore is primarily through building on this advantage. Tariffs would only reduce the purchasing power of Americans' wages. Small businesses and low-income households would suffer most from a high-cost economy.

Any economic damage would be compounded, of course, if our trading partners retaliated against our tariffs by enacting barriers against us. Mr. Buchanan calls the desire to avoid retaliation "the counsel of fear and timidity. Had we followed it in the Cold War we would all be speaking Russian." This retort, while rhetorically effective, confuses commerce and war. He would be protecting Americans not from Soviet tyranny but from products they want to purchase. An "invasion" of cheap cars is not like an invasion of tanks; there's a difference between VCRs and ICBMs. A trade war that destroyed international commerce seems a high price to pay to prove America's toughness. Running on a jobs platform and then destroying jobs is ultimately not a clever political strategy.

Mr. Buchanan attempts to counter these economic arguments by invoking U.S. history. In an op-ed two years ago he wrote, "From Lincoln to Teddy Roosevelt to Coolidge, the GOP was the party of industry. It supported free markets at home, protected by a high tariff wall—with low taxes and little regulation. The Night Watchman State. This was the foundation of American prosperity, the formula that converted the small agrarian economy of 1800 into the greatest industrial power the world had ever seen by 1900." But America's vast internal market had more to do with the country's success than tariffs did. The most protected industries, like sugar and textiles, were uncompetitive. And other industries paid the price of that protection: the high price of protected steel decimated the merchant fleet.

What may understandably appeal to Mr. Buchanan (and other conservatives) about the last century's protectionism, however, is that U.S. tariffs were then an alternative to other taxes, notably the income tax. And, indeed, he has recently proposed raising tariffs in order to cut other taxes that he dislikes. He would replace income taxes on small business with a 10 percent tariff on all imports from Japan, allegedly an unfair trader; he would slash inheritance taxes and replace the revenue with a 20 percent tariff on Chinese goods. The goal is to move back toward tariff funding of the government. (Ironically, the income tax itself originated as a populist blow against the tariff, which first the South and later farmers and workers saw as oppressive.) By cutting some taxes and raising tariffs, Mr. Buchanan hopes to create "a new coalition of supply-siders and economic nationalists." He writes that his tax plan "marries the growth ideas of Ronald Reagan to 'The American System' devised by Hamilton and Washington."

Alas, the marriage he proposes is unlikely to be a happy one—and not just because he stands alone among Republican candidates in funding his proposed tax cuts with an anti-growth policy. His press release asserts that since Japanese imports are currently $125 billion, his tariff will yield $12.5 billion—a projection that assumes that his taxes will have no effect on consumer behavior. That's not just implausible; it directly contradicts the protectionist purpose of the trade barriers. The barriers can raise the revenues he seeks, or they can keep out imports that he believes harm the economy. They cannot do both. And they certainly could not finance anything even remotely approaching the size of today's government. Hamilton understood the difference between a revenue tariff and a protective tariff: in Federalist #21, he explained that such taxes "prescribe their own limit, which cannot be exceeded without defeating the end proposed." Only by eliding that distinction can Mr. Buchanan simultaneously appeal to union members and to anti-taxers.

Mr. Buchanan's tax proposals also have unsettling implications for foreign policy. A government funded by tariff revenue is extremely dependent on the actions of foreign governments for its financial stability. In the War of 1812, for instance, tariff revenues crashed because the U.S. went to war with its major trading partner. It therefore financed the war by printing money, which of course led to inflation and economic destabilization. The pattern repeated itself in World War I: a decline in tariff revenues was the reason the income tax was so quickly increased far beyond what anyone had envisioned. If the government became dependent on tariff revenue, foreign governments and companies wouldn't need to hire the lobbyists Mr. Buchanan deplores. They could stay in their own capitals and exert leverage on U.S. policy. Indeed, tariff funding of programs would turn domestic interest groups into foreign lobbyists by making their programs dependent on other countries' willingness to trade. It's hard to imagine a more anti-nationalist tax system.

Indeed, "economic nationalism" in general would divert foreign policy from more worthwhile priorities. It would be difficult to maintain an alliance with a country while simultaneously engaging in a painful trade war with it. It is often said that an economic policy based on the premise that the material interests of nations conflict with one another would be likely to lead to international hostility. What is less frequently remarked is that a protectionist world would also be more hospitable to command-economy dictatorships like the ones that have been America's enemies in this century. Such societies, unable to compete with property-based systems industrially, tend to generate trade goods through extraction. Limited world markets enhance the value of these goods. Thus, American policies of the 1970s that raised the price of energy played right into the Soviets' hands, while the reversal of those policies under Reagan created a foreign-exchange crisis that forced the Soviets to reform. (Following Mr. Buchanan's foreign-policy advice during the Gulf War would have meant an effective return to the '70s policy of high energy prices, this time for the benefit of lesser totalitarians.)

Mr. Buchanan's apparently shrewd use of economic nationalism as a strategy that "enables me to reach into Clinton's constituency" has hidden dangers. As Robert Novak wrote in *National Review* [Aug. 14, 1994], Goldwater and Reagan also tried to enlarge the conservative coalition, but without "consciously reaching out to a wholly new constituency with ideas that differed substantially from those of their rivals inside the party." Mr. Buchanan's new coalition might not remain dedicated to limited government for long—or indeed for short. Its position on trade suggests a cramped view of economic freedom. And already the effort to create this coalition is pulling him in a statist direction. His speeches these days imply that if we ended foreign aid we would not have to cut "programs for veterans, for the elderly, for the poor, for farmers." Like Robert Reich, he attacks wealth inequality.

The link between protectionism and expansive government is more than a matter of ideological affinities. Free trade forces governments to compete by allowing consumers and investors to vote with their wallets against government excess. When burdens on the private sector grow too heavy, economic activity moves to other jurisdictions. Trade barriers, however, shut off this escape route. (It was precisely in order to prevent this kind of regulatory competition that liberals demanded labor and environmental side-agreements to NAFTA; those side-agreements led some free-traders to oppose the whole package.) Mr. Buchanan complains—rightly—that federal taxation and regulation make it harder for American companies to compete with foreign ones. Yet instead of attacking the burdensome taxes and regulations, he would reduce the pressure to reduce them by shielding industry from their consequences.

Protectionism invites Big Government, Big Labor, and Big Business to form a coalition to socialize the economy; free trade protects ordinary citizens from all of them. Free trade is not just another issue to be bargained away for progress on OSHA regulations or on welfare. It is strategically important because it is a structural limit on government power. Protectionism, on the other hand, is a prerequisite for higher levels of regulation, spending, and taxes.

It would therefore undermine Mr. Buchanan's goal of political reform by giving government another set of favors to sell. As Joe Cobb of the Heritage Foundation explains, "A lot of the buying and selling of the Senate [in the 19th century] was due to tariffs." Whatever the argument for a particular breach of free trade—to help infant industries, to guard national security, whatever—any conceivable protectionist regime would soon become the plaything of politically powerful industries. That's not a hypothetical concern; it is once again increasingly the way U.S. trade policy is set.

In short, Pat Buchanan offers Americans a false economic nationalism—one that would cause the economy to contract, the government to expand, and foreign policy to be hobbled. Conservatives should stand for something better: a true economic nationalism, one that's confident of Americans' ability to compete in global trade without federal favoritism.

GRADING FREE TRADE[6]

Home Economics: In 1993 economist Gary Hufbauer of the Institute for International Economics testified before Congress that NAFTA would lead to an annual net gain of 170,000 jobs in America. President Clinton declared 200,000 jobs would be added "by 1995 alone." . . . Hufbauer estimated that the United States has suffered a net loss of 225,000 jobs under NAFTA. *Multinational Monitor* and Public Citizen's *Global Trade Watch*, an early NAFTA opponent, recently surveyed sixty-six major U.S. corporations that had claimed the trade agreement would cause them to create jobs or expand exports; fifty-nine reported that their predictions have not come true.

Mexican Studies: The minimum daily wage in the Mexican factories in the border area—the *maquiladoras*—was about $5 in 1993, before NAFTA. Now it is about $2.20.

Business Management: Transnationals taking advantage of the accord and the devalued peso can make out like bandits. Zenith, for example, estimates it will save $10 million in manufacturing costs in Mexico.

Macroeconomics: (No grade; the course was canceled.)

Natural Sciences: So far, the number of cleanup and water or waste projects funded by the environmental institutions set up under NAFTA side agreements is a whopping zero, while the growth of unregulated industry has led to further pollution.

Sociology: Up and down news for the Mexican edition of *Forbes*. There were eight billionaires in 1992. Two years later, with NAFTA, there were twenty-four. But too few invested in dollars, so now, after the peso crash, there are only ten.

Statistics: In 1993 NAFTA promoters deployed statistical models predicting that the U.S. trade surplus with Mexico—$1.7 billion in 1993—would balloon to $9 billion by the end of 1995. The trade *deficit* for the first nine months of 1995 was $12.2 billion, and for the entire year is projected to be $15 billion.

[6]Article by David Corn, from *The Nation* 262:19 Ja 1 '96. Copyright © 1996 by The Nation L.P. Co. Reprinted with permission.

Political Science: Since the accord, the ruling PRI's hold on the country has slipped. It has lost control of the economy, as firms have used NAFTA rules to break into various industries. Drug dealers and gangsters have gained more clout. The political scene is chaotic, but the accord has been a boost to the Zapatistas.

III. POLICY CONTROVERSY

Editor's Introduction

Global trade has despoiled the environment, divided nations, and facilitated the spread of crime and loss of jobs. Is there room for trivialities like bent bananas when jobs are at stake? The first article of this section, "Going Bananas: A Story of Forbidden Fruit," reprinted from *Commonweal*, follows the controversy over bananas with "abnormal curvature." Silly as it sounds, this debate has exposed significant political tension within the borderless European market. German officials have criticized France and Spain, the key beneficiaries of European Community (EC) regulations. Meanwhile, "The new tariff boosted banana prices . . . cut demand . . . resulting in a loss of several thousand jobs in fruit-importing businesses," the author asserts.

Our Canadian neighbors are the topic of Bill Montague's article, reprinted from *USA Today*. U.S. economists, businessmen, and financiers are concerned over Quebec's proposal to separate Canada, converting the province into an independent country. "If political and financial turmoil push [Canada] into a full-fledged recession, thousands of U.S. jobs could be lost," states Montague.

Under NAFTA, Mexican workers are finally gaining a voice and building solidarity. In "Laboring to Cross the NAFTA Divide," reprinted from *The Nation*, David Bacon, a freelance journalist, has described the Mexican union's resistance to NAFTA. It is made clear that crossing the border for jobs is essential. On May Day, 1995—Labor Day for most of the world—maquiladora workers and border activists demanded wage increases to compensate for the fall of the peso. San Diego's Support Committee for Maquiladora Workers, in cooperation with other committees, has organized workers to help them keep their jobs.

The fourth article, reprinted from *Ms.*, explains the expanded corporate rights in GATT that put workers, consumers, and the environment at a disadvantage. Mary McGinn, the author of

"How GATT Puts Hard-Won Victories at Risk," points out that many companies now look to repeal national, state, and local laws that limit business practices. She also describes how three non-elected members of the new World Trade Organization handle all complaints behind closed doors.

"Mass Immigration, Free Trade, and the Forgotten American Worker," an article by Vernon M. Briggs, Jr., examines the problems that are caused by immigration legal or otherwise. Briggs identifies the problem as too many "poorly educated job-seekers in an era when low-skilled jobs are rapidly disappearing." He also discusses inadequate changes in the workforce of the United States since the mid-1960s. He presents the problems—layoffs and plant closings in the U.S., pollution and worker exploitation in less-developed countries—that free trade has yet to overcome.

GOING BANANAS:
A STORY OF FORBIDDEN FRUIT[1]

Who would have ever thought the biggest trade issue in . . . [1994's] European Community (EC) negotiations in Brussels would be regulations about bananas? Bananas? After months of wrangling, the EC ruled in the fall of 1994 that, beginning in January 1995, all imported bananas must be "free of abnormal curvature" and at least 14 cm (5.5 inches) in length and 27 mm (1.1 inches) in diameter—unless they come from several former European island colonies. This was at the same time as the European Court of Justice in Luxembourg rejected the bid of Germany, Europe's biggest consumer of bananas, to overturn the EC regulation that gives preference to bananas grown in EC member countries (especially Spain and Greece) and former EC colonies. Germany, you see, imports most of its bananas from non-EC countries, especially Latin America.

The decision was a strong blow to Chancellor Helmut Kohl during October [1994's] German election campaign, from which

[1]Article by John Rodden, from *Commonweal* 122:4 Mr 24 '95. Copyright © 1995 by *Commonweal*. Reprinted with permission.

his party, the Christian Democratic Union (CDU), emerged with a scant 10-seat majority. Kohl had vowed that he would get the EC banana-import regulations liberalized.

The German outcry against both decisions was loud. Germany's EC spokesman warned that the ruling would "open the floodgates to protectionism." The German press gave vent to the popular outrage. In Munich, the respected Sueddeutsche Zeitung editorialized: "In Germany, a storm of indignation is brewing against the Brussels Commission." In Ulm, the *Suedwest Presse* summed up the reaction of the German Volk: "Germany is always being condemned . . . . How often other EC states manage to blind the Luxembourg Court with their national interests . . . . [But] we Germans will have to get used to the idea that we don't have any special status in united Europe."

What's going on here? What are we to make of the so-called EC "banana split"? Why are the Germans getting bent out of shape over banana symmetries, sizes, and quotas? We Americans take bananas for granted; we even trivialize them—we speak of playing second banana, being driven bananas, banana republics, and on and on. But bananas are no joking matter to Germans. In Germany, bananas are an impossibly overdetermined symbol, signifying justice, national self-determination, cultural pride, deprivation, prosperity, Communist tyranny, capitalist luxury, unity, and economic and even sexual freedom. Let me explain.

It turns out that banana politics bears deeply on the issue of German identity, reflecting Teutonic tensions both within and outside reunited Germany. For the early postwar generation, many of whom as children knew of bananas only through the reminiscences of their elders, the fruit still evokes memories of humiliation, deprivation, and even famine. Ever since hunger overtook war-torn, occupied Germany in the mid-1940s, when even basic foodstuffs were unobtainable, bananas have symbolized luxury to both West and East Germans. This began to change in West Germany with the Wirtschaftwunder [economic miracle] of the late 1950s and '60s. Parents delightedly weaned their infants on "Banana Salad" baby food, the Gerbers of West Germany. Older West Germans still recall with pride the dramatic speech of Chancellor Konrad Adenauer in July 1957, when he brandished a banana at the Bundestag podium and hailed the fruit as "paradisiacal manna." Adenauer had just returned in triumph from a four-day filibuster in Rome, having finally gotten

"Protocol Number 10"—which guaranteed West Germans tariff-free bananas in unlimited quantities—written into the founding Treaty of the European Economic Community (EEC), predecessor of the present-day EC.

The story in East Germany was very different, and consequently the timing of . . . [1994's] European Court ruling came at a particularly cruel moment. After the war, bananas were simply absent from East German life—except as a special treat, courtesy of Castro's Cuba, at Christmas time (a holiday never officially recognized in the atheistic GDR). Bananas were regarded as a Western delicacy; their absence came to symbolize communism's failure to provide simple pleasures taken for granted in the West. Even through the 1980s, bananas were virtually unavailable to ordinary GDR citizens. Indeed, before the Wall fell, visiting West Germans often brought a feast of bright, ripe bananas to their East German relatives as a house gift.

When the Berlin Wall crumbled in November 1989, the banana became for Easterners an unofficial symbol of German unity and liberty. By 1992, East Germans were consuming nearly twice as many bananas per year as West Germans. Jubilant East Germans sported bumper stickers featuring two bananas forming the letter "D" for Deutschland. It all seemed a sign of better days to come.

Indeed, the Eastern lust for bananas soon symbolized more than just economic liberty. How deep had the banana slipped into the German psyche? Well, Der Stern reported that, according to a survey of East German sex shop sales in 1990, a banana shaped vibrator and a banana-flavored condom known as the "Wild Banana" led all other brands. But the banana passion soon turned ugly and began to divide, not unite, Germans. West Germans soon began referring to their naive countrymen in the Wild East as "Bananen." East Germans, in turn, resented West German "banana politics." After the March 1990 elections in East Germany, the last Communist ambassador to the U.S. angrily attacked Chancellor Kohl for interfering in the East German elections. The CDU had attracted crowds in the East by handing out free bananas; castigating Western consumerism, the ambassador attributed the CDU victory to "two months of banana policy."

Since 1989, Chancellor Kohl has turned bananas into a test case for European unity and for his conservative, free-market doctrines. During 1990–93, the single major policy issue concerning tariffs in the EC involved reunified Germany's obsession with bananas. Germans, who consume twice as many bananas as do citizens of any other EC nation (and more than 45 percent of total EC consumption), insisted on continuance of the special, duty-free treatment for German banana imports established in the 1958 Treaty of Rome protocol and contrary to the general guidelines of the 1990 Treaty of Rome.

And so, when the EC voted in February 1993 to impose quotas and a high tariff on non-EC-grown bananas, indignant Germans protested. Stickers in shop windows and car windshields urged, in Gothic script, that patriotic Germans "Esst deutsche Bananen!" ["Eat German bananas!"]. As a disgruntled German EC representative groused: "Why should Germans enthuse about the EC, when we see what the Community is doing to our bananas?"

The EC "banana split," as journalists quickly tagged the controversy, exposed the sharp political tensions underlying the move toward a single, borderless European market. Protesting everything from the EC ban on bent bananas to the neomercantilism of France and Spain, German trade officials pressed their case. They publicly attacked France and Spain, whose banana-growing former island colonies have been the chief beneficiaries of the newest rulings. The new EC import regulations aim to help banana growers in European tropical islands (e.g., France's Martinique and Guadeloupe, Spain's Canary Islands) and in former European colonies. But Germany, which lost all its colonies after World War I, complains that Germans prefer larger, bright yellow, Latin American "Dollar Bananas"—so named because of their size and rich color—to the more expensive, smaller, paler "Eurobananas" from EC overseas territories and former colonies.

German officials also warned that the new tariff would not only send banana prices skyrocketing and reduce German banana imports, but destroy the economies of several Latin American banana-exporting nations.

And some of the dire predictions have borne fruit: The new tariff boosted banana prices 63 percent in 1994 and cut demand by more than 25 percent, resulting in a loss of several thousand jobs in fruit-importing businesses. Moreover, with German banana imports from Latin America down 50 percent in the latter half of 1993, 170,000 jobs in Latin America vanished.

For Germans, the banana has become the symbol of the EC's hypocritical refusal to act on its free-trade rhetoric. For much of the rest of Europe, the banana shootout with Germany represents a necessary attempt to prevent reunified Germany from throwing its weight around and gaining a "special status" based on its economic superiority. But whatever the odds, Bonn has vowed to continue the fight against Eurobananas and for "Dollar Bananas."

In short, the banana split is likely to deepen.

CANADA TEETERS ON BRINK[2]

Canada is teetering on the edge of a political upheaval that could send powerful shocks through the U.S. economy and financial markets.

. . . Residents of Quebec, Canada's second-largest province, could vote to tear apart the USA's huge northern neighbor.

On the ballot: a referendum granting Quebec's separatist government authority to secede from the 128-year-old Canadian federation, transforming the predominately French-speaking province into an independent country.

Recent polls show an extremely close race, with independence supporters clinging to a razor-thin lead. Those results have produced something close to a state of shock in the rest of Canada. . . . Most analysts had assumed a majority of Quebec residents ultimately would reject the secession option, as they did in a 1980 vote.

That still could happen. But at the moment, politicians, investors, and business executives on both sides of the border are being forced to confront the ugly possibility that a secession vote will lead to a messy divorce, followed by an even messier divorce settlement.

That unpleasant thought sent Canadian stocks, bonds, and the Canadian dollar tumbling . . . [in one day], with the Toronto 300 Stock Index losing nearly 3 percent, its biggest one-day loss since October 1989. Financial markets recovered slightly . . . , but most analysts say the calm could prove short-lived, if polls continue to indicate a secessionist victory.

[2]Article by Bill Montague, from *USA Today* 1A O 25 '95. Copyright © 1995. USA TODAY. Reprinted with permission.

"The whole thing is an absolute nightmare," says Martin Barnes, managing editor of *Bank Credit Analyst*, a Montreal-based newsletter. "We could be looking at an economic and financial Bosnia."

At stake for the USA:

Economic growth. Canada, with its twenty-eight million people and $548 billion economy, is the USA's largest single trading partner. Canadians bought $115 billion in U.S. exports [in 1994] . . . and sold $131 billion worth of goods and services to the USA.

The U.S. and Canadian auto industries are highly integrated. About $74 billion in cars and parts cross the border each year.

But Canada's economy already is sputtering. If political and financial turmoil push it into a full-fledged recession, thousands of U.S. jobs could be lost.

A secessionist victory also could push the Canadian dollar into a deep slump, making U.S. products more expensive in Canada and Canadian products cheaper here. That, too, could cost U.S. jobs.

[On October 24, 1995] . . . the Bank of Canada—Canada's equivalent of the U.S. Federal Reserve—raised short-term interest rates almost one full percentage point to defend the Canadian dollar. That will mean higher rates on Canadian mortgages and consumer loans. That's likely to slow the economy even more.

Debt. Canada is deeply in shock, and U.S. investors are the nation's largest creditors. Canada's federal government has about $484 billion in debt outstanding, and U.S. investors—including a number of major mutual funds—own an estimated 10 percent to 15 percent of it. Quebec itself has $38.4 billion in debt, and nearly 20 percent is owned by U.S. investors.

If Quebec leaves, the status of all that debt is in doubt. Quebec leaders say they're willing to assume a "fair share" of the national debt. Who would decide what's fair?

"It's all a legal no-man's land," says Carl Weinberg, chief economist for High Frequency Economics, a consulting firm. Canadian Finance Minister Paul Martin has vowed the federal government would stand "100 percent" behind the country's debt. But a Quebec secession could deprive the Canadian government of more than 20 percent of its tax revenues.

Trade. Thanks to the North American Free Trade Agreement, Canada and the USA enjoy almost unlimited access to each other's markets. But legal scholars agree: An independent Quebec wouldn't automatically be covered by NAFTA. An abrupt rise in tariffs could cause serious disruptions in U.S.-Quebec trade—no minor matter considering that Quebec accounts for more than 20 percent of Canada's total economic output, and by itself is the USA's ninth-largest trading partner.

Investment. U.S. businesses have major stakes in both Canada and Quebec. General Motors Canada, for example, is the province's largest single company and employs about 3,500 Quebec residents.

Officially, most U.S. companies aren't taking sides in the election.

"It's up to the people of Quebec to decide their future," says Stewart Low, spokesman for GM of Canada. But most make it clear they regard the idea of an independent Quebec with unease. "We feel Canada would be far better off if it were to remain intact," says Tony Fredo, vice president of Ford of Canada.

Also nervous: residents of U.S. towns and cities that border Quebec, who depend heavily on economic ties with the province. Peter Clavelle, mayor of Burlington, VT, says retail sales to Canadians and visits by Canadians already are down because of the weak Canadian dollar.

One big unknown: the probable economic policies of an independent Quebec. Leaders of the province's ruling Parti Quebecois have staked out clear—and controversial—positions on many cultural issues, such as promoting the French language and French culture, and encouraging French-speaking families to have more children. But their economic views are more obscure.

Some English-speaking Canadian analysts are dubious. Ihor Kots, of the Canadian Bond Rating Service in Montreal, predicts Quebec Premier Jacques Parizeau would support aggressive government intervention in the economy and favor Quebec's powerful trade unions. "He's said he is prepared to be very different from the rest of the world," Kots says. "I think you have to be concerned."

Even if Quebec chooses secession, it may find it hasn't gained much room to craft an economic destiny, analysts say. An independent Quebec would be relatively small (it's economy is about the size of Massachusetts') and saddled with debt.

"It would have among the highest deficits in the world, both on a per capita basis and as a percentage of Gross Domestic

Product," Kots says. In the end, Quebec could find itself at the mercy of global investors and forced to make brutal cuts in social spending and wages in order to avoid default or hyperinflation.

Quebec's separatist leaders "are not stupid, and I think they understand what the economic obstacles would be," says Ross Preston, managing director of WEFA Group Canada, a consulting firm. "But they are acting with their hearts, not their heads."

Quebec Important to Canadian Economy

In Canada, 26 percent of the population lives in Quebec. At 594,860 square miles, it is the second largest of Canada's ten provinces and two territories. It is more than twice the size of Texas.

Economy. In U.S. dollars, Quebec's provincial debt of $52.5 billion compares with Canada's national debt of $661.2 billion. Quebec produces 22 percent of Canada's gross domestic product.

LABORING TO CROSS THE NAFTA DIVIDE[3]

Tijuana, Mexico—In 1994 the Labor Department certified 17,000 applications (out of 34,000 received) for unemployment extensions for U.S. workers who lost their jobs because of NAFTA. . . . [In 1995] there were 35,000 applications in the first nine months alone. The actual number of NAFTA-caused job losses is undoubtedly much higher, given chronic underreporting. And with the battered peso, things aren't expected to improve soon, as Mexican labor grows cheaper and cheaper and Mexicans lose jobs in even greater numbers.

As we enter the second year of NAFTA, anyone in the labor movement who may once have been cool to the idea of cross-border cooperation is beginning to realize its absolute necessity. The question is how, and with whom? Slowly, both answers and problems are presenting themselves.

[3]Article by David Bacon, freelance journalist and photographer, from *The Nation* 261:572–4 N 13 '95. Copyright © 1995 by The Nation L.P. Co. Reprinted with permission.

The idea is certainly not new. The Flores Magon brothers planned the first battles of the 1910 Mexican Revolution with support from the Wobblies in St. Louis and Los Angeles, and paid for it—specifically, for threatening U.S. mining interests—with imprisonment and death in Leavenworth. In the heady days of the C.I.O., Vicente Lombardo Toledano and Latin American labor radicals built ties between progressive union federations from Canada to Central America. These traditions were largely forgotten after World War II, as the A.F.L.-C.I.O.'s international department fought the cold war on the labor front for the U.S. government, promoting friendly climates for corporate investment and doing their best to neutralize or eliminate radical and independent unions throughout the world. After NAFTA, U.S. workers felt the full impact of the international department's disastrous betrayal. Forty-five years of cold war politics in Mexico had built no relationships based on solidarity. If they wanted a common front with Mexican workers, or those in other countries, they would have to build it from scratch.

Tijuana is a good place to see what is stirring.

"You can imagine how desperate we are. Here, if you have no money, the government won't enforce the law. We really have very good laws in Mexico, but a very bad government."

Veronica Vasquez spoke those words as she stood in the middle of a dusty street here amid a raucous demonstration for the dignity of women in the maquiladoras. Before she was fired, Vasquez worked at Exportadora de Mano de Obra (literally, Exporter of Labor), a captive contractor of National O-Ring, a division of American United Global Corporation, in Downey, CA. Exportadora employed 180 at wages of $20-$40 a week.

. . . [In 1994] at the company's summer picnic the women workers were forced to participate in a "bikini contest" for the enjoyment of company president John Shahid. When the women balked, they were told that he wanted to videotape the contest. Fearing for their jobs, they agreed.

Afterward, workers protested and asked for improvements in wages and conditions. When they met with Shahid, Vasquez recalls, he took $15 from his pocket and threw it on the table: "We told him we didn't want money like that, so he asked us what we would give him in exchange. We said we'd give him our work, but he told us that he wanted love."

The women at Exportadora filed sexual harassment charges with Tijuana's public prosecutor. Two days later, the plant was closed. The workers then filed suit in Los Angeles Superior Court, with help from San Diego union activists on the Support Committee for Maquiladora Workers. This is the first time workers in Mexico have filed suit in a U.S. court on charges like these. But the backlash came quickly. Once the suit was filed in Los Angeles, Exportadora workers who had found jobs in other maquiladoras were dismissed. Earlier, when workers at another factory, Plasticos Bajacal, tried to organize an independent union, shop-floor leaders there were fired and blacklisted as well. Now maquiladora workers in Tijuana are afraid to organize openly.

Workers and their supporters have changed tactics to organize and survive on the job. The San Diego committee now cooperates with the Border Workers Regional Support Committee (CAFOR), a group of maquiladora workers and Tijuana activists. They hold meetings for workers and residents of communities in the factory zones. Health and safety experts come down from California to explain how to recognize health hazards. At the Sanyo maquiladora on Otay Mesa, one of Tijuana's largest plants, CAFOR helped workers survey hazards and successfully press for improvements. In Chilpancingo, below Otay Mesa, where many maquiladoras are located, they are educating community residents. A closed battery-recycling plant sits on the mesa's edge, where lead and heavy-metal deposits have been measured at concentrations 40,000 times over acceptable levels. In 1993, six children in this small barrio were born without a brain, a condition called anencephaly. . . . [In 1994] thirteen more children were born this way. Chilpancingo is now one of several border communities discovered to have clusters of anencephalic births. Two others are Matamoros/Brownsville and Del Rio, on the Texas border.

"We of course blame the companies for this," says Eduardo Badillo, CAFOR's secretary for coordination, "but we don't hold them alone responsible. Our own government shares the responsibility for these conditions because it doesn't insist that the factories abide by the laws and regulations which already exist. These companies don't come to this side of the border just to eat tacos and enchiladas."

Over the past two decades unions and union activists in the United States have supported strikes by miners in Cananea and

Nacozari, electronics workers in Tijuana and factory workers in Juárez and Matamoros. In the early 1990s, Teamsters from the closed Green Giant plant in Watsonville, CA, chased the work from their plant to Irapuato, where they tried to help the Authentic Labor Front, or FAT, organize the new work force. Closer to the border, the United Electrical Workers formed a partnership with FAT, the only union federation in Mexico that spoke out strongly against NAFTA. They targeted Juarez plants of General Electric, many of whose U.S. plants have U.E. contracts.

At G.E. the U.E. and FAT gained enough support among workers to demand a union election. In response G.E. fired a number of union supporters and threatened others with a shutdown and blacklisting. The union lost the vote. In Chihuahua, a FAT effort to organize at Honeywell led to the firing of dozens of workers. No election was ever held.

These incidents prompted the first two complaints filed under NAFTA's labor side agreement. A hearing was held by the National Administrative Office in the U.S. Labor Department, set up by the treaty to receive complaints, but the N.A.O. recommended no action.

A third complaint was brought before the N.A.O. [during the] fall [of 1994] . . . by the Coalition for Justice in the Maquiladoras, the International Labor Rights Fund (I.L.R.F.), the American Friends Service Committee and Mexico's National Association of Democratic Lawyers. It was filed on behalf of workers at Sony's maquiladora in Nuevo Laredo, south of Texas. In April 1994 Sony fired eighteen workers who had tried to run for office in the plant union, a branch of the government-affiliated Confederation of Mexican Workers (C.T.M.). After the firings, work stopped. Sony brought in riot police, who beat workers and forced them to return to their jobs. The workers lost the election, then organized an independent union in the plant and tried, unsuccessfully, to register it with the government. In this case the N.A.O. issued a report on the firings, company intervention in the election, police violence and the Mexican government's refusal to give legal status to the independent union. U.S. Labor Secretary Robert Reich met with then-Mexican Labor Minister Santiago Oñate on the last point, and agreed only to pursue an academic study of the problem of registering new unions in Mexico.

In July [1995], Sony workers made a second attempt to register their union. Again the Mexican labor board refused to recognize it. Jerome Levinson, lead attorney for the I.L.R.F. in the case, called Reich and Oñate's agreement "cynical in the extreme."

A complaint was also filed in Mexico against the United States by the Mexican telephone workers union. It alleged that Sprint Corporation fired more than two hundred Latino workers in San Francisco, and shut down their workplace, a week before they were to vote for the Communications Workers of America in a scheduled union representation election. Again, Reich and Oñate met to discuss the case, but no change has taken place in the status of the fired workers.

Meanwhile, for ordinary Mexican workers, life has become terribly hard. President Clinton found $20 billion to bail out (mostly U.S.) investors, but Mexican workers are paying for it with their standard of living. Prices have risen at least 42 percent since January [1995]. A worker at the Zenith television factory in Reynosa, on the border with Texas, now earns a weekly average of 135 pesos, or $19.27. Bus fare to work is 3.5 pesos. Juan José Delgado, a member of the Comité Para Todos Todo in Tijuana and an activist in the opposition Democratic Revolutionary Party, accuses the government of "legalizing slavery, with a minimum wage the equivalent of $2.50 a day." He points to an increase in child labor in Tijuana as well.

If Mexicans here try to cross into San Ysidro, CA, they confront a ten-foot iron wall extending east along the border, U.S. economic and trade policies push them to immigrate, but its immigration policies punish them when they do.

"Solidarity among workers should cross the border as easily as companies move production," says Mary Tong of the San Diego committee. On May Day maquiladora workers and border activists tried to bring the idea to life, as they organized demonstrations to demand a wage increase to compensate for the fall of the peso. Some 100,000 people filled the Zocalo, Mexico City's central plaza, making the same demand. They came even though the C.T.M.'s Fidel Velasquez, bowing to a request by President Ernesto Zedillo, decided not to hold a May Day parade, breaking a seventy-four-year tradition. But workers took to the streets anyway. In Tjiuana, despite fear of firings and the blacklist, workers from the maquiladoras formed a 1,000-strong march from the outskirts to downtown. They demonstrated as well in Juáez, Matamoros, Piedras Negras, Ciudad Acuña, and Nogales.

Border demonstrations were reinforced by a march and rally in San Antonio, TX, led by eight fired Sony workers. In New York City, the Interfaith Center on Corporate Responsibility, representing 275 religious institutions with investments worth an estimated $45 billion, announced that it was introducing shareholder resolutions at AT&T, Ford, General Motors, G.E., Johnson & Johnson, Zenith, and other corporations. The resolutions call for companies to raise the wages in the maquiladoras.

The cross-border movement is still too new to see clearly which tactics will be most successful. But whether organized by unions or by looser networks of workers and activists, it heads in the right direction. Unlike Lane Kirkland's old cold war approach, these efforts build solidarity from the bottom up, with democracy and mutual respect, and are based on fighting corporations and the policies of their political allies. And they allow workers themselves a voice.

HOW GATT PUTS HARD-WON
VICTORIES AT RISK[4]

The bigger the economy gets, say free trade proponents, the higher incomes around the world will rise and the lower prices will fall. A global market means global prosperity. But in the case of the General Agreement on Tariffs and Trade (GATT), bigger appears better only for the heads of big business. The 125-nation trade deal, which the U.S. ratified in late 1994, dramatically expands corporate rights at the expense of workers, consumers, and the environment.

Under GATT, tariffs—essentially taxes on imported goods—will be reduced by as much as 36 percent over the next decade. As with the North American Free Trade Agreement

[4]Article by Mary McGinn, North American regional coordinator for Transnationals Information Exchange, from *Ms.* 5:15 Mr/Ap '95. Copyright © 1995 by *Ms.* Magazine. Reprinted with permission.

(NAFTA), which took effect in early 1994, tariff reductions open domestic markets to foreign competition. Lower tariffs also make it cheaper for manufacturers in industrialized countries to set up shop in countries where labor costs less. Such changes have meant accelerated job loss in the U.S. during NAFTA's first year, particularly in the garment industry, where women workers are the majority. And as a result of GATT, the Amalgamated Clothing and Textile Workers Union estimates that upward of a half million textile and garment jobs are at risk. Women also make up the majority of workers in other vulnerable industries, such as food processing and data entry.

A reduction in tariffs also means the world's largest tax break for multinational corporations, resulting in sizable revenue losses for governments. In the U.S., Congress is proposing several ways to make up for the estimated $13.9 billion that will be lost, such as cuts in an already underfunded federal pension program. While Republicans and Democrats alike cry for a reduction of the federal deficit, GATT only puts the U.S. further in the hole.

But GATT's most insidious feature is that it makes it much easier for corporations to push for "deregulation"—the scrapping of any national, state, or even local law that places restraints on their business practices. Such restraints can be environmental laws like a ban on asbestos, limits on the use of child labor, a mandatory minimum wage—or even affirmative action and pay equity policies. Antidiscrimination measures benefiting women and other disadvantaged groups may be considered unfair restraints on a company's right to hire whom it wants, for the hours it wants, at the right price. In essence, free trade agreements level the corporate playing field by pushing labor, health, and environmental standards to the lowest common denominator.

The European Union, for example, has made it clear that it has a problem with the U.S.'s new law requiring all food manufacturers to list complete nutritional content on labels. Under GATT, the union can now lodge a complaint with the new World Trade Organization (WTO), a lofty name for a body administered by three nonelected regulators. These "trade experts" will consider complaints submitted by any GATT member-country that views a particular law in another country as an obstacle to free trade. So the European Union can argue that because most European food manufacturers aren't required to label their foods as specified under U.S. law, the law serves to keep European goods off U.S. shelves. Instead of adopting its own consumer protection laws, the European Union will most likely appeal to the WTO to have the U.S. law modified, or even overturned. If the U.S. refuses, it will be charged steep fines, unless it can convince a majority of GATT member-countries to override the WTO decision. Keep in mind that WTO tribunals are closed to the public and press. As consumer advocate Ralph Nader has written, the WTO mandate is a "staggering rejection of our due process and democratic procedures."

Unfortunately, most U.S. women's advocacy groups took no position on GATT. But clearly, all women have a lot to lose: expanded freedom for multinational corporations jeopardizes social justice everywhere.

MASS IMMIGRATION, FREE TRADE, AND THE FORGOTTEN AMERICAN WORKER[5]

If continued mass immigration and the pursuit of free trade result in undermining the nation's trade union movement and its labor-protection laws, then the price is too high. It must also be considered exorbitant if these policies continue to help reduce American workers' living standards and widen income inequality within the nation.

There have been two discretionary changes in U.S. economic policies since the mid-1960s that have caused fundamental changes to occur in the workforce of the United States.

The first, affecting supply conditions, has been the accidental revival of the phenomenon of mass immigration from out of the nation's pre-industrial past by inadvertent changes in its immigration policies. Mass immigration had been the original means by which the United States acquired and built its urban labor force during the 19th and early 20th centuries. That era came to an end in 1914. It was due, initially, to the events associated with World War I and, subsequently, to legislation passed in the

[5]Article by Vernon M. Briggs, Jr., professor of Economics at the New York State School of Industrial and Labor Relations at Cornell University, from *Challenge* 38:37 My 1 '95. Copyright © 1995 by M. E. Sharpe Inc. Reprinted with permission.

1920s. Only the year before—in 1913—the revolutionary concept of assembly-line production had been introduced in the United States. This dramatic advance in technology launched the nation into an era of mass production and rapid industrialization, which have characterized its economic development ever since. From 1914 until the late 1960s, immigration declined steadily—in terms of its effects on the size and composition of the American workforce and of its significance to the U.S. economy.

The second change, affecting demand conditions, has been the adoption of free-trade principles as the basis for the conduct of the nation's international trade. Until the 1960s, the United States had never adhered to such practices. The domestic economy had been built behind high protective tariff walls for almost two hundred years. There was no previous experience in U.S. history to demonstrate what might actually happen were it to follow this policy course. There was only the rhetoric of free-market advocates to describe what might happen in a setting based on idealized assumptions about how competitive markets theoretically operate.

Theoretically, the benefits of free trade are based on the premise that its pursuit will cause income distribution changes to occur within each trading nation. But, as Lester Thurow has poignantly written: " . . . average incomes will go up with free trade, but there will be millions of losers in each country . . . . The theory simply maintains that the losses of the losers will simply be smaller than the winnings of the winners." The losers, in the contemporary case of the United States, are those unskilled and poorly educated workers who, under protectionism, were able to secure jobs—sometimes even with high wages. Disproportionately, they are workers from minority groups. Those in the manufacturing sector have been especially vulnerable. The winners are high-skilled and better-educated workers who often are employed in service industries. Thurow also notes that " . . . the theory assumes that the winners will compensate the losers so that everyone in each country has an incentive to move to free trade but in fact such compensation is almost never paid." With the exception of a few provisions for retraining some displaced workers, there are no compensation provisions in any of the new trade policies adopted by the United States.

The 1960s

In the 1960s, at the time the initial steps were taken to alter the prevailing immigration and trade policies, there was no recognition of any relationship between the two policy initiatives. The nation still basked in the unparalleled benefits of the economic prosperity of the post-World War II period. Real income was rising sharply and income inequality was being reduced. Looking back, it is clear that no one anticipated what was about to happen to the American workers as the direct result of those discretionary actions taken by their own federal government in both of these key policy areas.

While elements of immigration policy in the early 1960s were topics of continuing controversy, the attention of reformers was focused primarily on the means of selection, not on the level of immigration. The most contentious issues in immigration policy debates at the time centered upon efforts to terminate the Mexican labor program (the infamous "bracero program"), and on the controversy over the right of border commuters (i.e., "green-carders") to work in the United States, even though they continued to live in Mexico.

Indeed, the significance of immigration in American life and the American economy had been declining for more than forty years. The number of foreign-born persons in the United States in 1970 (9.6 million people) was lower in absolute terms than at any previous (or subsequent) time in the 20th century. Moreover, its percentage of the total population (4.6 percent) in 1970 was also at a level lower than at any previous or subsequent time in U.S. history. With the initial wave of the "baby boom" generation just reaching the primary labor-market entry age of 18 years in 1964 (a phenomenon that would continue to supply record numbers of labor-force entrants for the next sixteen years), there was no prospect of a labor shortage on the nation's horizon.

The goals of the civil rights movement came to fruition in the 1960s. Its activities culminated in the passage of the Civil Rights Act of 1964, with its historic equal employment opportunity provisions. With the adoption of this landmark antidiscrimination legislation, and with the active pursuit of an expansionary fiscal policy (i.e., the broad-based tax cuts that also had been enacted in 1964), we were confident we would reduce unemployment. The adoption of a broad array of inclusive human-resource development programs by the Johnson administration began to prepare black workers for the jobs the new *Great Society* was about to create. Tight labor-market conditions would force employers to hire blacks—now protected by equal opportunity laws. The newly enacted human-resource programs would assist them to become qualified to compete for such job openings.

When the Immigration Act of 1965 was passed, it too was seen as part of this broad-based effort to eliminate the last vestiges of overt discrimination from American public policy. It was also seen as an integral part of the nation's civil rights agenda. Immigration reformers attacked the explicit ethnocentrism of the national origins admission system, which had been put in place in 1924 and had continued since that time. Certainly, there was no intention to increase the level of immigration. The reformers sought only to eliminate the overt discrimination that was embodied in the extant legislation. Indeed, the floor manager in the Senate for the Immigration Act of 1965, Edward Kennedy (D-Mass.), stated unequivocally during the final floor debate that "this bill is not concerned with increasing immigration to this country; nor will it lower any of the high standards we apply in selection of immigrants." Subsequent events, however, have shown that his expectations were wrong on both counts. The 1990 Census revealed that the foreign-born population (which totaled 19.7 million persons as officially measured, but which undoubtedly missed many more who had entered illegally) had more than doubled the level reported only twenty years earlier in the 1970 Census. Moreover, the skills and education of those immigrants entering since 1970 have been found to be considerably below those of earlier waves of immigrants at similar stages of assimilation. The incidences of poverty, unemployment, and welfare dependency among them were also higher than was true of earlier immigrants. And their labor-force participation rate was lower than earlier waves. Another era of mass immigration to the United States had commenced and, like its predecessor, it mainly involved people who lacked human-capital endowments. It was the low-skilled segment of the U.S. labor force in general, and the minority work force in particular, who bore the brunt of their competition.

With respect to trade policy, we seem to have forgotten that the economy of the United States was not built on the basis of "free trade," or on anything else even barely resembling that concept. In fact, the nation's rise to world economic prominence was based precisely on the fact that it did not depend upon its control of foreign markets. Rather, it produced its own goods for its vast home market. Foreign competition was largely prohibited. Tariffs were first enacted in 1789 against certain foreign imports as a means to provide revenue for the newly established nation. Alexander Hamilton, the first U.S. Secretary of the Treasury, had proposed an even more extensive system of tariffs to protect the nation's infant industries. Initially, his advice went unheeded. But during the War of 1812 with Great Britain, U.S. industry flourished when foreign trade was cut off due to a British naval blockade of the coastline. Following the American victory in that war, business interests gained sufficient political control to have protective tariff legislation imposed on most imported goods. Their efforts were joined by western farmers, who also favored protection from foreign competition for their agricultural products. Thus, the Tariff Act of 1816 was adopted. It was the first purely protective tariff legislation in U.S. history. But it was far from the last.

The Tariff Act of 1824 expanded the coverage of goods and raised the rates. Similar steps were taken again in 1832. There were some downward revisions in the rates in 1833. But they were raised and the coverage was expanded again by the Tariff Act of 1842. In part, the Civil War itself was fought over the tariff issue. The Whig Party of the North (later to become the Republican Party) strongly favored tariffs. The other party (called Republicans at the time, but later to become the Democratic Party) was split over the issue. Members from the South were opposed to tariffs, while members from the North and West were in favor of tariffs. The subsequent defeat of the South in the war not only meant the end of slavery, but the end of the opposition to tariffs for many decades to come.

Tariffs remained high into the 1880s. During the election of 1888, in fact, the subject was the major issue of the presidential campaign. The Republicans won. President Benjamin Harrison led Congress to enact the McKinley Tariff Act of 1890. It raised tariffs to the highest levels in U.S. history. It also extended coverage to goods never before covered. A substantial reaction to this legislation ensued. But by the time Congress finished with it, the "reform" legislation—the Wilson-Gorman Tariff Act of 1894—actually expanded the existing protections. The presidential election of 1896 also centered on tariff issues. William McKinley's defeat of William Jennings Bryan meant another victory for tariff supporters. Subsequently, the Dingley Tariff Act of 1897 raised tariffs again to new heights. There were efforts to modify some of the tariffs in 1909, but they resulted in the enactment of only minor revisions. President Woodrow Wilson (who was elected partly because the Republican Party was split over tariff policy in the presidential campaign of 1912) succeeded in gaining passage of the Underwood Tariff Act of 1913. It significantly lowered existing tariff rates. These reductions, however, had a short life. Not only did World War I inhibit trade, but tariffs were again raised (following the war) by the Emergency Tariff Act of 1921. And they were raised again by the Fordney-McCumber Act of 1924.

When the depression hit the U.S. economy in 1929, Congress responded by passing the infamous Smoot-Hawley Tariff Act of 1930. It raised U.S. tariffs to historic heights. The significance of the passage of the Smoot-Hawley Act, however, was not that it involved the imposition of tariffs (as was mischievously suggested by Vice President Al Gore in his 1993 television debate with Ross Perot over the efficacy of NAFTA), but that it raised tariffs just another notch above their already high levels.

It was with the election of President Franklin Roosevelt in 1932 that the United States began the process of altering its tariff posture. A new position was established. It involved the principle of reciprocal tariff reductions that would be determined through bilateral negotiations between the United States and other nations on an individual basis. You cut your tariffs on specific goods, and we will cut ours. But before any significant changes could occur, World War II interrupted the process. During the war years, foreign trade came to a virtual halt. But the productive capabilities of the United States were dramatically increased. Moreover, the productive capabilities of all the other major industrial nations of the world were destroyed during the war. The United States emerged from the war as the leading industrial power on the planet. In 1950, it accounted for 50 percent of the world's total production of goods and services.

From this position of strength and dominance, the United States slowly began abandoning its protectionist tradition. It was to its economic advantage to do so. The United States was instrumental in the adoption in 1947 of the General Agreement on

Tariffs and Trade (GATT). Forty signatory nations (including all of the industrial powers of the noncommunist world) pledged to reduce the tariff barriers to world trade. At the time, it was understood that a parallel agreement among GATT members settling minimum labor standards for wages and working conditions would soon be negotiated. It would assure the creation of minimum labor standards which would establish criteria for the conduct of the new international trading arrangements. But to this date, the international labor standards agreement has yet to emerge.

It was not until the early 1960s that the actual process of tariff reduction began. In 1962, the United States enacted the Trade Expansion Act. It permitted President John F. Kennedy to enter into negotiations that could lead to tariff reductions of up to 50 percent of their existing levels. It also authorized the President to participate in the GATT negotiations—to be held in Geneva in 1964. These talks were subsequently called the "Kennedy Round"—in honor of the president, who had been assassinated the year before.

In the early 1970s, this process suffered a brief setback when President Richard Nixon imposed a 10 percent surtax on all imported manufactured goods to the United States. But in 1980, the election of President Ronald Reagan brought into office a Republican president who was committed to reducing government involvement in free-market operations. In contrast to his party's heritage, he was a strong advocate of free trade. Further GATT negotiations began in 1986. They covered a broader range of agreements in such areas as copyrights, software, investment services, and the ever-thorny issue of agricultural subsidies. These talks—known as the "Uruguay Round"—ultimately reached final agreement among the 107 signatory nations in late 1993, and were formally signed in Marrakech, Morocco in April 1994. It was also in 1993 when the United States signed NAFTA with Canada and Mexico. NAFTA seeks ultimately to eliminate tariffs on trade among these three nations.

Trade and Immigration Policy Development

With regard to trade and immigration policy development, therefore, the United States has passed through three distinct periods. Each deserves a brief review:

Mass Immigration and High Tariffs. The first period commences at the time when the United States actually began to function as an independent nation in 1788. It lasts roughly to when World War I broke out in Europe in 1914. During that time, as discussed earlier, the United States had the consistent experience of using tariffs to protect its business and agricultural enterprises. It was a period of generally escalated tariff rates and broadened coverages. But in the labor market, it was a period of virtually unrestricted immigration. Thus, the labor market functioned under conditions of nearly unlimited competition, while the product market was comprehensively sheltered from most foreign imports. The net result was the stimulation of domestic competition.

During this era, conditions for workers were uniformly deplorable. "Sweatshops" flourished. Wages were low. Long work days were standard. Unsanitary, unhealthy, and unsafe working conditions were virtually universal. Child labor was commonplace. Employment discrimination was widespread. It was also a period that witnessed frequent spells of cyclical unemployment without any income maintenance provisions for those who lost their jobs. The few efforts to establish trade unionism during this era were generally unsuccessful—except in a few skilled crafts, and in the railroad industry. Even these unions had to straggle to survive. Under these conditions, business interests generally prospered and dramatically expanded in scale.

Low Immigration and High Tariffs. The second stage extended roughly from 1914 to the mid-1960s. It was the period in which mass immigration essentially came to a halt. But tariffs continued to be broad in coverage, to rise (through 1933), and to remain high.

Essentially, the nation's initial experience with mass immigration ended in 1914. Would-be emigrants from Europe could not leave. Immigration from Asia had been largely restricted by exclusionary laws enacted in 1882 against the Chinese and by a "gentleman's agreement" with Japan. But Asian immigration from the Philippines (which was a U.S. colony from 1898 until 1946) continued, until it too was sharply restricted in 1934. When World War I ended in 1918, immigration pressures from Europe showed signs of returning to their prewar levels. This process, however, was quickly halted by temporary legislation in 1921 that became permanent three years later with the passage of the Immigration Act of 1924. It was also called the National Origins Act, due to the discriminatory admissions system it enacted favoring immigrants from Western and Northern Europe, but disfavoring or prohibiting immigration from everywhere else in the Eastern Hemisphere. It also imposed a ceiling on Eastern Hemisphere immigration for the first time.

With the exception of the depression decade of the 1930s, however, the United States experienced the most prosperous period in its economic history during these years. Real income soared in the 1920s, and again throughout most of the post-World War II period, through the decade of the 1960s. Over this period, the United States created a variety of high-wage jobs that became the envy of the world. In the process, the nation developed a massive domestic market—especially for expensive but technologically advanced goods and services produced by its highly heterogeneous industrial structure.

It was also during this time that the nation began to enact a broad range of worker-protection laws and social-insurance systems to remove some of the harshness of working and living in a competitive society. These ranged from laws dealing with minimum wages, maximum hours, child-labor bans, unemployment compensation, food stamps, Aid For Dependent Children, Social Security, Medicare, and occupational health and safety. It also included federal government support for the establishment of a system of collective bargaining to resolve workplace disputes between labor and management. Membership in trade unions soared to include about one of every three workers in the 1950s. The initial steps to end overt discrimination were also enacted in this era.

With the exception of the depression years, this era (for the most part) was the most prosperous in U.S. history. Not only did production levels soar, but employment levels, living standards, and business profits did as well. The disparity in the distribution of income among American families also was reduced.

Mass Immigration and Low Tariffs. The contemporary era began in the mid-1960s. It has been marked by the resumption of mass immigration and a sustained effort to reduce tariff rates and coverages. Putting aside the many platitudes associated with immigration and free trade, the fact is that the nation has now entered into uncharted waters. So far, if the standard for judgment is the impact on the American worker, the signs are not encouraging.

There has been a marked upward trend in the nation's unemployment rate since the mid-1960s. The unemployment rates of the mid-1960s were in the mid-3 percent range. In every succeeding period of prosperity since that decade, the unemployment rate has tended to be higher than in the preceding prosperity period. The annual unemployment rate has not been below 5 percent since 1970. Those worst affected by this secular trend of gradually rising unemployment have been the less-skilled workers. And their ranks are disproportionately composed of minorities, youth, and women.

But even worse have been the effects of what the macroeconomist Wallace Peterson has identified as declining real family incomes. This downward trend began in 1973, and has continued to this day. Studies that have focused on trends of real earnings show that they too have been falling since 1973. But the losses have been the greatest for those with the least education. The U.S. Bureau of the Census, for example, reported in 1991 that white males aged 25 to 34, with less than a high school diploma, experienced a 42 percent decrease in real earnings from levels that existed in 1973. High school graduates sustained a 31 percent decrease in their earnings. Those with some college have experienced a 21 percent decline in earnings. Even college graduates have seen a 14 percent decrease in real earnings. For women and nonwhites, the declines have been even more pronounced. Although studies that focus specifically on the effects of immigration on earnings are sparse, there is specific evidence that the immigrants of the 1980s have exerted a negative influence on the wages of native-born workers who have low skills.

The nation's poverty-stricken population has increased from 31.7 million in 1988 to 36.9 million in 1993. The percentage of Americans living in poverty in 1993 (14.5 percent) was the highest recorded for any one year since 1983, when it was 15.2 percent. In other words, while the percentage of the population living in poverty declined slightly after 1983, it has been rising again in the 1990s. In fact, the data for 1993 reveal that poverty increased three times faster that year than did the overall population.

Given these trends, it should come as no surprise that the distribution of family income in the nation became distinctly more unequal during the decade of the 1980s. The lowest one-fifth of all families in the United States saw their share of all income decline from 5.2 percent to 4.6 percent between 1979 and 1989. The top one-fifth of all families saw their share of all income increase from 41.5 percent to 44.3 percent. The top 5 percent of all families saw their share increased from 15.3 to 17.4 percent during this period. As for the state of trade union members, their numbers have been contracting since the 1960s. By 1992, fewer than 16 percent of the labor force were union members—about one-half the percentage of the 1950s.

Even worse has been the increase in reported violations of the nation's worker-protection laws in the 1980s and early 1990s. Accounts of the revival of child-labor violations, the return of "sweatshops," and extensive fair-labor-standards abuses abound in urban areas—especially in those communities inundated by the recent waves of immigrants, who are themselves often the victims of such exploitation. It is also clear that the economic status of urban blacks is deteriorating in the wake of the onslaught of immigrant competitors and the rapid erosion of the urban job base—due, in part, to the effects of free-trade practices.

Imperatives for Policy Change

Certainly, there are other factors that cause the aforementioned conditions. The differential employment impact of computer-based technology would rank alongside the adverse effects of the new trade and immigration policies. There are also the demographic effects having to do with the "baby boom" generation and the women's movement. They both have contributed to the unprecedented increases in the labor force we have witnessed during this period. Defense cutbacks have also caused dislocation effects—the result of the unexpected end of the Cold War in 1991 and of shifting consumer spending preferences toward services. But this is precisely the point. The labor market is in a state of rapid transformation with regard to the industrial, occupational, and geographic changes in employment patterns. Many of the causative influences are beyond the capacity of public policies to control. Policymakers can only try to respond in effective and compassionate ways. But immigration and trade policies are purely discretionary actions. In this period of rapid economic change, they both should be shaped to serve the national economic interest. Neither can be said to be so shaped today.

The preeminent domestic economic problem facing the United States in the 1990s is what to do with the rapidly increasing surplus of unskilled and poorly educated job-seekers in an era when low-skilled jobs are rapidly disappearing. Pending welfare reform proposals by the Clinton administration—for example, to force more than two million adult welfare recipients to go to work—cannot possibly be taken seriously unless something is done to stop the inflow of unskilled, poorly educated, and largely non-English-speaking immigrants (especially those who enter illegally) into low-skilled urban labor markets. And we must reduce the incentives for firms that hire significant numbers of low-skilled workers to move abroad or shut their doors, because they cannot compete with foreign imports.

Indeed, the plight of low-skilled workers in this country is so ominous that I deem three public policy proposals mandatory, if we seriously care about the welfare of these workers:

First, the nation's legal immigration system must be mended to prohibit the admission into the United States of unskilled adult workers as immigrants or nonimmigrants, regardless of the admission category. The only exception would be for spouses.

Second, it is mandatory that steps be taken to tighten the enforcement of the nation's immigration laws with respect to illegal entry and the abuse of the political asylum system by economic refugees.

Third, it is essential that public policy identify those occupations (especially in the goods-producing industries) that continue to employ low-skilled workers (e.g., in garment manufacturing and in agriculture). We need to impose significant tariffs on foreign imports into these industries as a way to prolong the ability of the U.S. firms who produce similar goods to stay in business.

If anyone has better ideas, they desperately need to be brought forth into the arena of public debate. But this nation cannot rely on the standard homilies of free market advocates that, somehow, the market will adjust to these radically new employment patterns. To the degree that it does, it will do so with extreme human cruelty and will increase the likelihood of worsening social tensions.

The mass-immigration and free-trade movements are part and parcel of a broader movement toward a laissez-faire economic environment. Its goal is to reduce the discretionary role of government to influence economic outcomes, leaving those outcomes to be caused by invisible market forces. But market forces have traditionally manifested little concern for worker rights, human welfare, or environmental protection. These forces are insensitive to the difficulties often experienced by individuals, their families, or their communities to adjust to such unfettered decisions.

Under the free-market paradigm, markets are assumed to be efficient. Hence, any interference in their operation is alleged to be a departure from perfection—no matter how humane, compassionate, or wise such interference might seem to be. But if one starts from the opposite assumption—that markets are not inherently efficient—interventions in an imperfect world can improve the conditions of life and welfare of both individuals and nations.

We require an immigration policy that is flexible in the number of people it allows to enter the United States legally each year. Likewise, one that admits people primarily on the basis of the human capital endowments they bring (and that the U.S. labor market seeks) is needed. In other words, the nation's immigration policy ought to be accountable for its economic consequences. The present system is not. It must be a policy that is firm in the certainty that its terms will be enforced against illegal entry and refugee abuse. It must also contain provisions that allow U.S. employers to hire nonimmigrant foreign nationals in only the most extreme labor-shortage situations.

In addition, the trade policy of the United States must be required to meet the same standard. Its provisions must serve national interests, and not special interests. The fundamental rationale for trade between nations should be to raise real living standards. It should not be to contribute to an erosion of existing work standards, or to a loss of employment opportunities. Neither should it allow pollution of any nation's environment, or provide a vehicle for employers in advanced nations to exploit workers in less-developed countries for competitive gain.

Currently, neither U.S. immigration nor trade policies can be said to meet the standard of being designed to raise the real living standards of American workers. Indeed, in their present forms, they both represent the opposite of that goal. Simply stated, the welfare of workers is not a priority of either. Only the private financial interests of influential sectors of the business community are being served by the present policies.

It is past time for working people and those who empathize with their welfare to see to it that both of these discretionary policies be changed from their present forms. If continued mass immigration and the pursuit of free trade result in undermining the nation's trade union movement and its labor-protection laws, then the price is too high. It must also be considered exorbitant, if these policies continue to help reduce American workers' living standards and widen income inequality within the nation.

IV. A WORLD OF INDECISION

Editor's Introduction

All countries involved with global markets have seen both advantages and disadvantages to foreign trade. More recently, free trade—or at least less protectionism—has become the popular choice. However, not all countries are enthusiastic about the new World Trade Organization (WTO), and the United States, which has solved some of its trade problems through bilateral and unilateral agreements, tops the list. The first article, by Jeffrey E. Garten, reprinted from *Foreign Affairs*, examines the main concern of foreign leaders: the United States finding other means to solve its free trade dilemmas. Garten is aware that European countries deal with other free trade alternatives all the time. He discusses many countries, from Brazil to Japan, arguing that the United States' ability to dictate the rules that everyone could agree on has "become more and more vital."

In November 1995, an economic summit heard China's pledge to cut tariffs in 1996. Andrew Pollack's article (reprinted from *The New York Times*) reveals that China has pledged to cut tariffs on "more than 4,000 items by an average of at least 30 percent." China's promise has served as a catalyst for eighteen other Pacific-rim countries who envision regional free trade by the year 2020.

The next article, "Economic 'Miracles,'" by David R. Henderson, compares the trade policies of India and South Korea to illustrate the successful traits of each; Henderson includes both productive and stagnant economic trends. While his example involves various other countries, he hopes the U.S., particularly, will learn from the past. He calls for less government regulation, which "hampers not only freedom but also economic well-being."

In "Barbarian Horses at the Gate," Japan is described as a protectionist country that is beginning to see certain advantages to free trade. Edmund L. Andrews describes the horse-breeding situation in Japan and the effects foreign trade has on gambling and the breeding industry, which has been traditionally dominated by the United States.

The last article, by Michael Rogers, reprinted from *The Economist*, explains how South Koreans believe that it is unpatriotic to buy imported goods. South Korea's popular choice is still a protected market; however, the South Korean transportation department has reconsidered a plan to allow foreigners to build a high-speed railway. An economist from Seoul fears that, in equating patriotism with protectionism, his fellow countrymen "have lost sight of an open market as being in their own best interest."

IS AMERICA ABANDONING
MULTILATERAL TRADE?[1]

Commitment to a New World Trade Order

In two years of travel for the Clinton administration in Asia, Europe, and Latin America, I have found foreign leaders' most recurrent concern to be that America is moving away from its historically strong support for the multilateral trading system. Rather than embrace the new World Trade Organization (WTO) and bring all its trade disputes before that body, the United States, they charge, is trying to solve its problems through bilateral agreements at best or unilateral fiat at worst. This substitution of the law of the jungle for established international rules, the critics say, encourages unbridled mercantilism, protectionism, and heightened political tension between countries, weakening global trade.

Set aside for a moment the hypocrisy of Europeans who deal bilaterally all the time, and the behavior of Japan, which continues to practice highly managed trade that runs directly counter

[1]Article by Jeffrey E. Garten, Dean of Yale University's School of Management, from *Foreign Affairs* 74/6:50–62 N/D '95. Copyright © 1995 by Council on Foreign Relations. Reprinted with permission.

to the spirit of the WTO. The fact is that ministers from Canada, Brazil, Korea, India, and Singapore, European Union commissioners, and business leaders from Toronto to Hong Kong are saying that the United States is turning its back on the multilateral trading system. The accusation is particularly significant in light of the past half century of American support for the General Agreement on Tariffs and Trade (GATT), the predecessor of the WTO. During this time the United States led every major round of global liberalization, providing the ideas and political muscle to bring negotiations to a conclusion and, most important, keeping American markets open in good economic times and bad so other economies could stay afloat. No other country came close to exercising this role.

Serious as the indictment is, it is also wrong. The issue is not whether the Clinton administration fully supports multilateralism, because it certainly does. The more relevant question is, what kind of multilateralism?

No Longer a Luxury Good

Many remember the days when America was so wealthy that it could subordinate economic and commercial policies to the goal of strengthening its political alliances. They recall that before the 1990s, GATT negotiations were as much designed to keep the West united and prosperous in the face of the Soviet threat as to expand trade for its own sake. They yearn for an America that accorded the process of developing multilateral trade rules the same importance as the results those rules yielded. That era, however, is over.

Today the United States supports multilateralism because it is in its commercial interest. The administration does not spend a lot of time worrying about holding the free world together, as the momentum everywhere is toward democracy and capitalism. But this does not mean the stakes in building an open trading system based on laws and regulations are any lower, or the urgency any less. American commercial interests are vast—north, south, east, and west—and the United States needs the tangible benefits of multilateralism in the marketplace.

After all, the most ubiquitous multinational companies are American, and most of them are globalizing their production in ways that require trade liberalization across many countries simultaneously. The United States also has the world's most open market, which means it gains enormously from multilateral commitments made by others en masse: it is a lot easier for us if everyone liberalizes agricultural quotas or government procurement procedures at once than if we have to slug it out country by country.

Moreover, expanded trade is now more critical to America's future than at any other time in this century. Exports and imports together have more than doubled since 1970, from 11 percent of GDP to 23 percent. In the last two years exports have increased by more than $100 billion—more than the total exports of Australia, Sweden, or South Korea. If this trend continues, as Commerce Department economists believe likely, U.S. exports will climb from $650 billion in 1994 to $1.2 trillion by the year 2000.

Exports are woven into the job base as never before. A decade ago exports supported seven million American jobs. By the year 2000 Commerce Department projections show more than sixteen million jobs tied to sales abroad. And this is not ordinary work; it pays 15 percent more than the average manufacturing wage, carries benefits at least 30 percent higher than the average job, and is far less likely to be affected by slumps or corporate restructuring. Exports are vital to our economic future. With monetary policy constrained and no real alternatives to finance expanded federal spending, exports will loom larger than ever when the next downturn comes.

As bright as the export picture may be, the United States must achieve more. Most important, millions more high-wage jobs must be generated, not just in the interests of a vibrant economy but also for social cohesion. In addition, serious trade deficits will have to be offset. In 1995 the current account deficit could reach $170 billion, representing a continuous deterioration over the past several years. While as a percentage of GDP this is considerably less than in the late 1980s, it is still too large, requiring billions of dollars in borrowing each month, adding billions to America's indebtedness, and frequently raising concerns in currency markets. Increased foreign competition, particularly from Asia, is likely to keep up the pressure.

Add to this mix the fact that all our trade competitors—from Canada to Korea, Japan to Brazil, Germany to China—have accorded the highest national priority to increasing their exports, and it becomes clear that the stakes for the United States in having the right kind of multilateral trading system have reached new heights. We must, therefore, apply rigorous criteria in judging the system, supporting it, and attempting to shape it.

What America Wants

What is the right kind of multilateralism? The administration is not hooked on theory, ideology, or leftover Cold War sentiments. Quite simply, it is looking for workable procedures and rules within a reasonable time frame.

First, it wants greater openness on the part of other nations, such that their markets provide opportunities to the United States broadly equal to those the U.S. market provides them. The traditional trade barriers of tariffs and quotas must be lowered, but the administration is also attacking nontraditional barriers like the webs of government regulations that strangle competition and interfere with investment flows, lax antitrust enforcement, tolerance of collusive corporate behavior, blocked access to product distribution systems, and inadequate enforcement of intellectual property rights. Washington is concerned, too, about labor practices and environmental protection.

The administration wants to see more fair play in the ways that governments assist domestic firms in international competition for major projects. The United States is focusing on governments that provide below-market financing for their exports, condone bribery to win deals, and offer a host of other incentives to distort decisions of countries like India, Brazil, China, and Indonesia that are awarding big contracts for power plants, airports, and telecommunications systems.

The administration favors a multilateral approach to both market access and anticompetitive practices, and in fact the vast majority of its activity in trade is on a multilateral basis. Such efforts don't make headlines because they are slow, technical, and hardly as dramatic as *a mano a mano* fight. But since the end of the Uruguay Round global trade talks in December 1993, the United States has been foremost among those pressing GATT and then the WTO to further reduce tariffs and liberalize government procurement and to continue negotiations in telecommunications and shipping. The administration has proposed multilateral consideration of the environmental aspects of trade. It has gone to the WTO as a broker in trade disputes with Korea on agricultural products and Japan on whiskey taxes. In the Organization for Economic Cooperation and Development (OECD), it has strongly advocated multilateral rules for investment, an initiative against bribery, and international guidelines for trade finance.

On a regional level, no other nation has pushed harder than the United States to develop rules and procedures for freer trade in Latin America or among the Asia Pacific Economic Cooperation (APEC) countries. The United States also proposed the Transatlantic Business Dialogue with the European Union (EU) to focus attention on lowering barriers to trade and investment across the Atlantic, especially unreasonable standards on regulations, products, and quality and safety testing. The dialogue will begin in November with a conference hosted by the Spanish government and chaired by cabinet ministers and CEOs from the United States and Europe.

The Critics' Charges

If America's recent record of support for multilateralism is excellent, why is the country taking so much flak? The long list of foreign grievances includes Section 301 of U.S. trade law, which allows retaliation in the face of closed markets when negotiations fail; antidumping laws, which mandate higher tariffs on foreign products dumped in America at below-cost prices; and the "extraterritorial" reach of U.S. law, as in attempts to penalize foreign companies for violating U.S. trade sanctions on other countries. But these are long-standing complaints. In at least two of the areas—Section 301 and antidumping—the United States is now subject to WTO review as a result of the Uruguay Round. Extraterritoriality is a problem, often driven by Congress, and successive administrations have tried to contain it.

Foreign anxiety in fact centers on three high-profile examples of recent U.S. policy. They are the administration's dealings with Japan, especially on the automotive industry; the strong U.S. response this summer to an inadequate liberalization package in the multilateral negotiations on financial services; and the administration's aggressive help for American firms vying for big deals abroad. An examination of each case helps clarify the rationale for the administration's approach and shows that a potent multilateral trading system—one capable of coping with the problems and opportunities of this and coming decades—is always the ultimate objective.

Removing Japanese Roadblocks

In the case of Japan, the administration has several reasons for its emphasis on bilateral negotiations not only on autos but in areas ranging from government procurement of telecommunications equipment to insurance regulations.

When President Clinton and Prime Minister Kiichi Miyazawa agreed to establish the U.S.-Japan Framework for Economic Cooperation in July 1993, both wanted to handle a series of issues bilaterally; this was not an instance of American arm-twisting. In addition, the administration believes that many of the barriers in Japan—lack of antitrust protection, interlocking relations among companies that block entry by foreign firms, collusion between suppliers and manufacturers, and suffocating regulations—are not yet within the competence of the World Trade Organization, nor is there a consensus on creating and enforcing rules to deal with them. Along with intellectual property rights, such practices constitute the most important category of trade problems for the United States—far more substantial than traditional tariffs and quotas. Although Japan may be the most significant example, similar barriers exist from South Korea to Germany.

It will take the WTO many years to develop adequate laws on such barriers. Not only does the new organization have its hands full with traditional trade problems, but the above barriers are deeply rooted in the history, culture, and institutions of their societies. And the wide variations from country to country make multilateral liberalization much more difficult to achieve than with tariffs and quotas, where common numerical targets could be set. The United States cannot afford to wait that long. The trade pressures are too great, as are the temptations for other nations to emulate Japan.

This is where the auto negotiations came in. They were a full-court press by the United States to break through entrenched Japanese trade barriers beyond the current ambit of the world trade body. The administration took aim at the highly regulated market for replacement parts, the cartel-like behavior of Japanese car companies and their dealers, and the collusion between parts suppliers and automakers. After two years of strenuous negotiations, including a threat from the United States to impose a 100 percent tariff on Japanese luxury cars, the two sides in June [1995] reached a series of agreements that should lead to an opening of the Japanese automotive market. The WTO could not have adjudicated these matters in a remotely comparable time frame—certainly not in this decade.

The administration justifies such bilateral deals in other ways as well. Identifying and dealing with nontraditional trade barriers establishes a precedent on which multilateral law can build, just as the environmental and labor talks with Mexico can be guideposts for the WTO, which is now taking up those issues. Moreover, as Japan opens its market, every other country is eligible to compete for the benefits. In other words, the United States and Japan negotiated a bilateral agreement but the results were multilateralized. That is exactly what happened with the agreement between the United States and China on intellectual property rights earlier . . . [in 1995]. As soon as the ink was dry, the agreement's provisions were available to the EU, Japan, and all other comers.

Financial Services: A Half-Empty Glass

The abstention of the United States from the financial services agreement that was concluded in July [1995] under the auspices of the WTO in Geneva illuminates another set of considerations. The administration wanted a multilateral pact to liberalize trade in banking, insurance, securities trading, and fund management. The United States, after all, has the world's most competitive and sophisticated financial services industry and its market in the field is already the most open, so its firms stand to benefit most when other governments lower their barriers. Indeed, closed markets are costing us dearly in terms of jobs, projects for our companies, and the international competitiveness that comes with having our banks in all foreign markets. Even with closed markets in many countries, the United States exported more than $8 billion in financial services in 1994, but this is a pittance compared with its potential. For two years, therefore, the administration negotiated hard, but in the end did not feel that other countries' offers on liberalizing their markets satisfied its goals. The EU said, "Take half a loaf, it's better than nothing." The administration disagreed. It did not want to grace the insufficient offers of other countries with the imprimatur of a multilateral agreement that would have required U.S. commitments to automatically allow all foreign firms into the American market even if their home governments kept our companies out. We may choose to let them enter, but we need not make an irrevocable legal commitment to do so.

The United States should not be expected to sign any multilateral agreement placed in front of it. Our standards of openness are higher than others' because our market is more open. We want foreign countries to come up to our level, not to settle for the lowest common denominator. In any event, this is not the end of the issue. Where the administration feels foreign financial markets are too closed it will press bilaterally, and it will reserve the right to keep out of the American market new entrants from these countries until we have a fair deal. At some point the overall environment will be more open and thus conducive to a meaningful multilateral arrangement—which remains Washington's objective.

Playing Hardball to Help Our Firms

The administration's stepped-up support for U.S.-based companies seeking contracts overseas has elicited concerns abroad. Europeans in particular are critical. While not denying that they engage in such practices—how could they, since they've been at it, as have the Japanese, openly and not so openly, for a century— they seem to believe either that the United States is acting too aggressively or that we, as the world's major economic power, have a special responsibility "to abstain in the interest of the global economic system," as they often put it. A world in which companies can compete directly with one another is our strong preference, but it will not happen soon, especially if the United States walks off the field and wrings its hands on the sidelines.

Japan, Germany, Britain, and countries in a host of emerging markets from Taiwan to Brazil are expanding government support for their firms. The companies will be competing for, among other things, a piece of the more than $1 trillion in infrastructure projects planned in Asia, Latin America, and the Middle East. The Clinton administration has concluded that it does no good to call for a truce in government support for firms; that has been tried for years and no one will listen. While it pleaded in vain, the United States lost an enormous amount of business and jobs. The only choice now is a reluctant one to play the game as hard as the others so far as most kinds of support go, including financing, high-level trade missions, and political intervention by ambassadors, cabinet members, and even the president. (Bribery, of course, is not an option for the United States, for ethical and legal reasons. In Germany, to take one counterexample, bribes are even tax deductible.)

The Clinton administration and its successors will inevitably continue to play hardball in helping American firms lock up contracts abroad. Foreign governments will learn that the United States will not roll over when confronted with their aggressive tactics, and at the same time the cost of intervention will rise for them. The objective is to get all governments to behave more reasonably and recognize the folly of competing with one another to deplete their treasuries. It is too early to say whether this course is succeeding, although there is some positive evidence. Foreign leaders are protesting, which shows they are at least more bothered by the costs of their usual approach. In addition, in many instances in which the U.S. government has offered, as a defensive measure, to match through its Export-Import Bank below-market financing of foreign export credit agencies, those agencies have withdrawn their subsidized offers. Maybe this is a start on a real truce.

Multilateralism for the 21st Century

In this brutally competitive environment, moving toward as advanced a multilateral system as possible should remain our objective. The United States should continue to push regional free trade areas in Latin America and Asia. These arrangements can be the building blocks for a stronger and broader multilateral trading system. A regional approach, such as the North American Free Trade Agreement, allows the United States to go further in some areas, including tackling the most intractable nontariff barriers, than the WTO with its 100-plus members can go at this time. It is essential, however, that all regional pacts conform to the basic principles of the world trade body so that they do not undercut negotiations that have already taken place at the global level.

Japan and China, because of their size, power, closed markets, and export prowess, pose the greatest dilemmas for the evolution of the multilateral system. In dealing with them, America must balance bilateral pressure with more harmonization with other countries' efforts. It will be essential for the United States to make more effectively multilateral the pressure on Japan in the Group of Seven, the WTO, APEC, and the OECD. As for China, which is not a member of the world trade body, the United States should work closely with the EU and Japan, make China more of a G-7 focus than it has been, and use the Asia-Pacific group to apply peer pressure on Beijing to further open the Chinese market and to abide by international rules. Bringing China into the WTO on commercially viable terms will give the multilateral system a boost and subject Beijing to a wide range of globally accepted laws. The United States strongly supports China's entry, but Beijing must still undertake substantial reforms and policy commitments before becoming eligible to join.

With China and other big emerging markets, the world needs a better multilateral framework for bidding for their megaprojects. Competition among firms acting on their own is desirable, but when governments intervene, their involvement must be circumscribed and opened to scrutiny. The United States, the EU, and Japan should at least attempt to bring under a single framework rules for export credits, bribery, use of foreign aid for commercial gain, and other nonmarket ways to win contracts (such as granting landing rights in return for purchases of aircraft, as some European countries have done). The United States will not unilaterally disarm, but it should be willing to do so multilaterally and reciprocally. The Commerce Department has made such proposals to the Europeans, but so far has gotten little reaction.

The U.S. Congress needs extensive education on the trading system, how it has evolved, and where this and successor administrations would like to take it. This is urgent because the Constitution entrusts Congress with the overall responsibility for trade policy, whereas in all other nations the executive branch directs trade. Congress historically has been highly skeptical of multilateral arrangements that limit U.S. flexibility. It alone vetoed the creation of the International Trade Organization, which would have created a comprehensive set of trade rules nearly a half century ago, and more recently it had a very hard time approving many provisions of the Uruguay Round that would have subjected the United States to multilateral rules, particularly for dispute resolution. The youth and domestic concerns of many WTO member nations have created a world trade body even more conducive to unilateralism than has been seen in some time. This endangers U.S. backing for the organization because Congress has the power to undercut a policy of multilateralism, no matter how firm the support of this or any other administration.

Congressional skepticism is mirrored by growing economic nationalism in Europe, where high unemployment now mixes with lagging technological capabilities and a preoccupation with the internal workings of the EU. It may be time for a vigorous new campaign to prod the development of the multilateral trading system.

The United States cannot, as it once did, play the heavy alone in this; it does not have the clout, and its agenda has become more complicated. Neither a self-absorbed European Union nor the financially strapped and psychologically unequipped Japan can play the role either. As for the new World Trade Organization, it is merely a reflection of its most powerful members.

Would it not make sense to create a small, international group of "wise men" that would present recommendations to the Group of Seven and the WTO on the next steps to strengthen the multilateral trading system? The group would be composed of distinguished members drawn from public and private life but all representing personal views. Such an effort would be particularly valuable if launched at the highest levels of several key governments, and if it rose above tactical trade issues to offer a vision of what the trading system should look like a decade or two hence and what would be needed to realize it.

Many questions cry out for answers and multilateral approaches. Where should the big emerging markets fit in? What issues do mind-boggling new technologies raise? What would a regime for open and fair global competition for megaprojects look like? How can antitrust issues be handled on a global basis? At a minimum, a report by such a group would go well beyond what governments, hobbled by their short-term perspectives, are prepared to contemplate, and set an important target. It would also contribute to public understanding of the challenges involved.

Finally, this administration and ones to come must improve their multilateral commercial diplomacy. The United States must learn how better to pursue bilateral policies with multilateral support and to achieve multilateral goals with bilateral reinforcement. A good analogy is arms control during the Cold War, when disarmament became a matter of high foreign policy. America's top technical experts and senior negotiators were not divided by different professional languages and cultures. Moreover, Washington reinforced its bilateral negotiations with extensive consultations with many governments not directly involved, and backed up its multilateral efforts with highly focused approaches to individual governments. We knew how to work the system, and we did it with sophistication and energy. Trade policy today demands a quantum increase in the number of diplomats who understand the intricacies of trade law as well as the methods of diplomacy.

An effective multilateral trading system becomes more important for the United States every day. During the Cold War America could throw its weight around, but its relative strength is declining. By the end of the decade both an enlarged European Union and an integrated Asian market will surpass the United States in GDP. As our ability to call the shots dwindles, rules that everyone agrees on become more and more vital.

Washington should do all it can to lead the way in this new era of trade policy, but a new trade order will not be created easily or quickly. If other governments are disturbed by U.S. policies, they would do well to reexamine their own. The sooner they embrace truly open markets, the sooner real, sustainable multilateralism will be achieved.

IN A MOVE TO OPEN ITS MARKETS,
CHINA PLEDGES TO CUT TARIFFS[2]

Osaka, Japan—In one of its most substantial efforts to open its markets, China said . . . that it would cut tariffs [in 1996] on more than 4,000 items by an average of at least 30 percent.

China's promise captured the spotlight on a day in which leaders of eighteen Pacific-rim nations endorsed a blueprint to achieve free trade in their vast region by the year 2020 using what they described as a new and unique voluntary approach.

"I believe the APEC meetings in Osaka were of historic significance in that they moved APEC from vision to action," said

[2]Article by Andrew Pollack, from *The New York Times* A11 N 20 '95. Copyright © 1995 by The New York Times Company. Reprinted with permission.

Prime Minister Tomiichi Murayama of Japan, referring to the Asia-Pacific Economic Cooperation forum.

To show their commitment, each nation announced a so-called initial action toward lowering its trade barriers. Rather than announcing bold new initiatives, however, many nations, including the United States, mainly listed actions they had already announced or taken.

While Washington has led the drive toward free trade, American officials explained that the United States had already taken many steps to open markets and now had less to do than other countries.

Other countries, including Japan, announced that they would speed up some tariff reductions that had already been approved. The big exception was China, which needs to bring its trading practices more in line with international standards to join the World Trade Organization. It announced several other measures in addition to the tariff cuts.

Vice President Al Gore, representing President Clinton, cautiously praised China's measures but said more would have to be done before the Chinese would be ready to join the World Trade Organization.

"This was a positive step down that pathway," Mr. Gore said. "There are others."

C. Fred Bergsten, a Washington economist and chairman of an advisory group to the economic forum, said "Thirty percent or more tariff cuts sound fairly impressive." But he said that more needed to be known, like what items will be subject to the cuts. He said China's tariffs average about 40 percent, so a 30 percent reduction is equivalent to about 12 percentage points.

. . . The Clinton administration handed China a detailed "road map" of what it must do to be eligible to join the World Trade Organization, the successor to the General Agreement on Tariffs and Trade. Chinese officials have reacted positively to the road map and appear to want to work with it, American officials said.

The eighteen leaders met in a guest house at Osaka Castle. They also tried their hands, somewhat awkwardly, at a traditional Japanese tea ceremony in the castle garden.

In what has become a tradition, the leaders dressed casually. At the 1993 meeting on Blake Island, near Seattle, leather jackets and scarves were in vogue. . . . [During 1994] in Indonesia the leaders wore batik shirts. . . . They generally wore blazers and no ties. They were also allowed to wear their shoes, something that would be unacceptable in most Japanese guest houses.

How successful the economic forum will be at achieving its goal of free trade by 2010 for developed countries and 2020 for developing countries will not be known for many years. The "action agenda" released by the leaders today includes only guidelines and principles.

A good hint of how serious they are will come at next year's meeting, in the Philippines, where all the nations will have to present their plans for dismantling their own barriers. While these plans will be voluntary, the forum's members will make sure they are roughly "comparable."

"The Asia preference is to do things in a looser, less institutional, less contractual manner," said Tommy T. B. Koh, Ambassador at Large for Singapore.

Such loose and regionally based approaches to trade liberalization might become more prevalent because negotiating a formal worldwide treaty, as was done in the Uruguay Round of GATT, has become enormously cumbersome.

"We are reinventing the way you do trade liberalization," said Joan Spero, the United States Under Secretary of State for Economic Affairs.

Malaysia's Prime Minister, Mahathir Mohamad, reiterated that the targets were not binding, saying, "We are not held down to this date."

In a sense that is true because there is no enforcement mechanism. Nor is the economic forum a true trade bloc like the European Union where member nations give up some of their own sovereignty.

That could mean that members will never completely end protection of certain industries. But by leaving things vague and voluntary, the forum was able to get off to a faster start on things that can be done.

"It makes the Uruguay Round look like a slowpoke," said Dr. Bergsten, the economist. He said that forum members were supposed to begin dropping their barriers on Jan. 1, 1997, only about two years after the goal of free trade by 2020 was set at last year's [1994] meeting in Bogor, Indonesia. By contrast, he said, the Uruguay Round took about eight years from start to the beginning of implementation.

Those who favor the forum's approach say the free trade goal, if not a legal commitment, is a political one.

"It was a voluntary commitment in that nobody had a knee in their neck," said Gareth Evans, Foreign Minister of Australia. "That combination of self-interest and peer group pressure will produce the results in the Bogor declaration."

ECONOMIC "MIRACLES"[3]

Our adventure in looking at economic "miracles" begins with a tale of two countries. Their names are withheld to increase the suspense. For now, they will be called country A and country B. In 1950, these two nations are similar in many ways. Measured in 1990 dollars, country A has a per capita income of $240; country B's is $550. Both countries are so far behind the industrialized world that most observers think neither can ever attain a comfortable standard of living, let alone narrow the gap.

Country A has a number of things going for it: ample natural resources, a huge domestic market, railways and other infrastructure that are good by Third-World standards, and competent judges and civil servants. Country B lacks all of these. Country A's savings rate is 12 percent of its gross national product (GNP), while country B's is an anemic 8 percent.

In the early 1950s, country A's government begins a policy of heavy government intervention in both international trade and domestic business. Not only does the government impose tariffs in excess of a hundred percent, but it also requires all importers to get permission to import, often refusing to give that permission. Moreover, country A's government imposes detailed regulation on each industry. Let's say that you run a company in country A and you decide that you want to increase production. You cannot just do so without a license from the government. You want to enter an industry, but you cannot do so without a license. You cannot even diversify your product line without a gov-

[3]Article by David R. Henderson, associate professor of Economics at the Naval Postgraduate School in Monterey, CA, from *Society* 32:59 S 1 '95. Copyright © 1995 by Transaction Publishers. Reprinted with permission.

ernment-granted license. And often the government refuses to grant these licenses.

"Why?," you might ask.

In 1967, one of the bureaucrats answers why. He says that, without the industrial licensing regime, this country would fritter away its resources producing lipstick. The economist who asks the question notes that the bureaucrat's hair smells like— Brylcream.

Country A's government also owns and runs entire industries: atomic energy, iron and steel, heavy machinery, coal, railways, airlines, telecommunications, and electricity generation and transmission.

What are the results of all this government intervention? By 1990, country A's income per capita is up from $240 to $350.

Country B's government, with fewer natural resources, less infrastructure, and a lower savings rate, pursues a different policy. It allows much freer trade. And, although it regulates industries, by comparison with country A, it is a model of laissez faire. The result? By 1990, country B's per capita GNP is $5,400, and country B did well in spite of a major war conducted there between 1950 and 1953.

Country A is India. Country B is South Korea. I remember when I was a child in the 1950s' being told to finish what was on my plate because people were starving in South Korea. And now, South Korea's economy is one of the envies of the developing world.

This tale of two countries is just one of many. Take East and West Germany between World War II and the reunification in 1991. Both were decimated by the war. The two nations had similar natural resource bases, culture, and education. But which country were people trying to leave for the other? And not just trying the way one might leave the United States to go to Canada, for example, but cutting through barbed wire at night, risking being shot at by soldiers with machine guns, risking drowning by swimming across rivers. People were desperate to leave East Germany and enter West Germany.

This was because people in West Germany were much freer, in every way, than people in East Germany, and this freedom had led, from the late 1940s through the early 1970s, to prosperity. We learned to take West German economic growth for granted in the 1960s. But West Germany's fate was no more certain than East Germany's after the war.

In 1947, the German economy lay in shambles. Food production per capita was only half its 1938 level, and the official food ration set by the governments occupying Germany varied between 1,040 and 1,550 calories per day. Industrial production was only one-third of its prewar peak. Most observers thought that Germany would have to be a permanent client of the U.S. welfare state. Yet only a few years later, growth in West Germany was so high that people began to talk about the German economic "miracle."

But what caused this so-called miracle? Here are the facts.

The West German "Miracle"

The Need for a "Miracle." The Allied occupation forces had inherited the comprehensive price controls that Hitler had imposed on the German people. All industrial prices, all food prices, and all rents were regulated by law. In November 1945, the Allied Control Authority, formed by the governments of the United States, Great Britain, France, and the Soviet Union, decided to retain Hitler's price controls.

Whenever the government imposes a maximum price control on a good that is below the competitive price, it causes a shortage of that good. The bigger the gap between the controlled price and the competitive price, the bigger the shortage. In the U.S.-occupied zone of Germany, controlled prices in May 1948 were only 31 percent above their 1938 level, which does not sound bad until one considers that the amount of money in the German economy—currency plus demand deposits—was five times its 1936 level. With money many times its previous level but prices only a fraction higher, shortages were pervasive.

Price controls on food made people desperate. Henry Wallich, a Yale University economist who was also to be a governor of the U.S. Federal Reserve Board, wrote in his 1955 book *Mainsprings of the German Revival*:

Each day, and particularly on weekends, vast hordes of people trekked out to the country to barter food from the farmers. In dilapidated railway carriages from which everything pilferable had long disappeared, on the roofs and on the running boards, hungry people traveled sometimes hundreds of miles at snail's pace to where they hoped to find something to eat. They took their wares—personal effects, old clothes, sticks of furniture, whatever bombed-out remnants they had—and came back with grain or potatoes for a week or two.

In transactions between businesses, barter was so widespread that in many firms a new job title was introduced — "compensator." A compensator bartered his company's output and some inputs for other inputs, and—this is the problem with barter—often had to engage in multiple transactions to do so. In 1947, the U.S. military estimated that one-third to one-half of all business transactions in the U.S. and British zones in Germany used barter.

Price Decontrols. Economists have understood for centuries the inefficiencies that price controls cause. One who understood this very well was Ludwig Erhard, a German free-market economist who had written a memorandum during the war laying out his vision of a market economy. His memorandum had made clear, at some personal risk, that he wanted the Nazis defeated. In 1947, the Allies, wanting non-Nazis for the new German government, made Erhard the main economic adviser to U.S. General Lucius D. Clay, military governor of the U.S. zone. Erhard advocated a quick currency reform and decontrol of prices.

After the Soviets withdrew from the Allied Control Authority, General Clay, along with his French and British counterparts, undertook a currency reform on Sunday, June 20, 1948. They shrank the amount of currency, substituting about 93 percent fewer Deutschemarks (DM), the new legal currency, for the old Reichsmarks. With the money supply contracted, there would be far fewer shortages because the controlled prices were now stated in Deutschemarks.

That same day, the German Bizonal Economic Council adopted, against the opposition of its Social Democratic members, a price decontrol law that gave Erhard authority to eliminate price controls.

Between June and August of 1948, Erhard decontrolled the prices of vegetables, fruits, eggs, and almost all manufactured goods. He substantially relaxed, or simply suspended enforcement of, other price ceilings.

Tax Cuts. The government also cut tax rates. A young economist named Walter Heller, then with the U.S. occupation forces and later chairman of President Kennedy's Council of Economic Advisers, wrote in 1949 that to "remove the repressive effect of extremely high rates, Military Government Law No. 64 cut a wide swath across the German tax system at the time of the currency reform." Individual income tax rates, in particular, fell dramatically. Previously the tax rate on any income over DM 6,000 had been 95 percent. After tax reform, this 95 percent rate applied only to annual incomes above DM 250,000. For the German with an annual income of about DM 2,400 in 1950, the marginal tax rate fell from 85 percent to 18 percent.

Positive Results. The effect on West Germany's economy was electric. Wallich wrote: "The spirit of the country changed overnight. The gray, hungry, dead-looking figures wandering about the streets in their everlasting search for food came to life."

The day after currency reform, Monday, June 21, shops filled with goods as people realized that the money they sold them for would be worth much more than the old money. The reforms, wrote Heller, "quickly re-established money as the preferred medium of exchange and monetary incentives as the prime mover of economic activity."

Absenteeism also plummeted. In May 1948, absenteeism had averaged 9½ hours per week; the workers had been too busy foraging and bartering. By October, absenteeism was down to 4.2 hours per week. Between June and December, industrial production rose by more than 50 percent. After 1948, output continued to grow by leaps and bounds. By 1958, industrial production per capita was over three times its annual rate for the six months in 1948 preceding currency reform and price decontrol.

What looked like a miracle to many observers was really not. Ludwig Erhard expected these results because he understood the damage that inflation, coupled with price controls and high tax rates, can do, and the large productivity gains that ending inflation, removing controls, and slashing high marginal tax rates can unleash.

These are not isolated examples. We have had over forty years of experience with various economic systems since World War II. All manner of political—economic systems have been tried: communism, socialism, fascism, mixed economies, and relatively free economies. Government interventions have included tariffs, government ownership, high tax rates, high government spending, detailed economic regulation by central authorities, and price controls. This diversity, and the years of experience and data that have resulted, make it possible to draw conclusions about which economic policies work and which ones do not. Following are some lessons based on forty years of experience from over one hundred countries.

Economic Policies to Avoid

Avoid Protectionism. A good (or bad) example of protectionism is illustrated by India. By the mid-1950s, Indian firms had to get permission to import components or capital goods, and the government imposed massive tariff rates on those imports that it did allow. These restrictions, combined with many others, caused massive inefficiency. The Indian Tariff Commission complained that everything made a noise in Indian-made cars except the horn. India's economy stagnated.

Then, in June 1991, in the midst of a foreign-debt crisis, newly elected Prime Minister Narasimha Rao and his finance minister, Dr. Manmohan Singh, an economist who had argued in favor of opening India's economy to the rest of the world, began to free the economy. Import controls, except for those on consumer goods, were dismantled, and in three years the highest tariff rates fell by almost half, to 65 percent. The government planned to lower tariffs to 25 percent within four years.

The results of these and other reforms have already been dramatic. Per capita gross domestic product (GDP) is growing at 2.5 percent a year. Exports in 1993 rose by more than 20 percent, to over $22 billion, and are expected to increase another 20 percent in 1994. Also, India, with a population of 900 million people, has forty million people with household incomes of over 900,000 rupees. Adjusted for purchasing power, such an income would be equivalent to $600,000 in the United States. India's middle class, now numbering 150 million, and with incomes of 30,000 rupees ($20,000 in U.S. purchasing power), is growing by 5 to 10 percent a year.

Similarly, one of the biggest economic success stories in South America, Chile, has also become one of the most free-trade countries in the world.

In the 1950s and 1960s, Chile was highly protectionist, with tariffs averaging over 100 percent. By 1972, socialist president Salvador Allende damaged trade by having the government take it over. Between 1961 and 1972, real GDP grew moderately, averaging 4.2 percent. In 1973, the year of the coup that toppled Allende, economic growth was -5.6 percent.

In desperation, the Pinochet regime turned to the so-called "Chicago boys," native Chileans who had studied economics at the University of Chicago under free-traders Arnold Harberger and Milton Friedman. From 1974 to 1979, trade was liberalized, with average tariffs falling to 10 percent. After two years of adjustment, 1974 and 1975, in which real GDP grew by 1 percent and -12.9 percent respectively, economic growth took off, averaging 7.2 percent a year between 1976 and 1981.

The Latin American debt crisis, along with a worldwide recession and the dramatic fall in the world prices of Chile's chief experts—among them copper—caused two more bad years for Chile's economy. In 1982, Chile's real GDP shrank by 14.1 percent. Chile's government responded by increasing protectionism between 1983 and 1985, and growth during those years averaged only 2.6 percent.

A new round of trade liberalization began in 1985, bringing average tariff levels down to 11 percent by 1991. Between 1986 and 1991, Chilean economic growth averaged 6.7 percent. Economists Rudiger Dornbusch of MIT and Sebastian Edwards of UCLA, both experts on Chile's economy, wrote, "For the second time in two decades, one speaks of a Chilean 'miracle.'"

What India and Chile learned the hard way is that protectionism stunts growth. Its opposite, an open economy, allows each country to specialize in producing the goods and services in which it has a comparative advantage, and protectionism removes some of the incentive to specialize.

Is this connection between free trade and growth general? Yes. In 1987, the World Bank issued a report that correlated performance of forty-one developing economies with their degree of "outward orientation." Outward orientation, contrary to what it sounds like, does not mean that government encourages exports; it means simply that government policies, on net, do not discourage exports.

Clive Crook, economies editor of *The Economist*, points out that there are two ways to have an open, outward-oriented economy. The simple way is that which is followed by Hong Kong: totally free trade, with no tariffs, no import quotas, and no subsidies for exports. The second, much more complicated way, is South Korea's: to impose tariffs on imports but offset these by subsidizing exports. In the latter case, imported inputs that are used to produce exports are penalized, but the penalty is offset by subsidies to exports. The former approach is easier. As Crook points out, the latter approach requires clever, well-informed—and, I would add, well-intentioned—policymakers, always a group in short supply.

The bottom line of the forty-one-country comparison is that on average, the more outward-oriented a country is, the higher its annual real GNP per capita growth. Between 1963 and 1973, the three most outward-oriented economies in the comparison were Singapore, South Korea, and Hong Kong. (Taiwan would have been fourth, but was not in the sample.) These three also, not coincidentally, had the highest growth of real GNP per capita. The comparison was almost as striking for 1973 to 1985. Singapore, Hong Kong, and South Korea stood first, second, and fourth, respectively, in growth rates of real GNP per capita. In short, a major reason for the success of the so-called Four Tigers—Hong Kong, Singapore, South Korea, and Taiwan—is that they avoided protectionism.

Crook points out one other important economic advantage of avoiding protectionism: It gives politicians less room to buy and sell favors. When the Indian government required businesses to obtain licenses to import, for example, which officials benefited? Those with the power to hand out the licenses, because they could take bribes in return. Similarly, the businesses that wanted the licenses spent resources in other ways to influence the outcome, resources that would not have had to be spent if permission had not been required.

While these losses from the creation and sale of privilege may sound small, they are not. Two of the world's leading trade and development economists have coined terms to describe this activity. Jagdish Bhagwati of Columbia calls it "directly unproductive activity," and Anne O. Krueger of Stanford suggested the term "rent-seeking." A more descriptive term is "privilege-seeking." It is no accident that these terms were coined by two economists who have studied Third World countries: The economic waste from competition for special privileges in some Third World countries can be a huge portion of GDP. A study of Turkey in the late 1970s found these costs to be 5 to 10 percent of GDP. Another study concluded that these costs, plus the costs from creating monopolies where competition would have thrived, absent import restrictions, were 3 percent of GDP in Mexico, 4 percent in the Philippines, 6 percent in Pakistan, and 7 percent in Brazil.

Avoid Price Controls. Virtually the whole economics profession rejects price controls. Swedish socialist economist Assar Lindbeck once asserted, "In many cases rent control appears to be the most efficient technique presently known to destroy a city—except for bombing." Lindbeck may have understated the case. At a press conference in the late 1980s, Vietnam's foreign minister, Nguyen Co Thach, said, "The Americans couldn't destroy Hanoi, but we have destroyed our city by very low rents. We realized it was stupid and that we must change policy."

Similarly, price controls in other developing countries have wreaked havoc. The reason is simple: If governments keep prices well below their free-market competitive level, suppliers have much less incentive to supply; demanders have an artificial incentive to demand more. The result is a shortage that gets worse the bigger the gap between controlled prices and the price that would have existed in a free market.

A student of mine from Indonesia, when asked what were the major things he learned in my public policy course, focused on one. He said that he had always wondered why so many rice fields in his country were no longer being used to grow rice and why Indonesia had switched from rice exporter to importer. He now knew the answer: price controls on rice. Indonesia's case is familiar in Third World countries. Many of those countries' governments, dominated by urban dwellers, impose price controls on agricultural crops and cause huge shortages, and then subsidize imports.

Ghana is another example. In 1957, before Ghana gained independence, it was the richest country in black Africa. It also had the best-educated population and was the world's leading cocoa exporter. Its income per person equaled that of South Korea at the time.

In 1964, Ghana's government gained independence. But not Ghana's people. Had the government's explicit goal been to destroy Ghana's economy, it could hardly have done a more thorough job. Ghana's leader, Kwame Nkrumah, nationalized industries, built useless and expensive monuments to government, and last but not least, imposed price controls.

The price control authority was a government marketing board to monopolize the purchase of cocoa. No cocoa farmer was allowed to sell to anyone else. Between 1963 and 1979, while consumer prices in Ghana rose by 2,200 percent, the price paid by the government's marketing board rose by only 600 percent. As a result, Ghana's farmers diverted much land away from growing cocoa and instead grew crops for subsistence.

The governments of Tanzania, Somalia, Nigeria, Mali, Madagascar, Cameroon, Niger, and Senegal also kept food prices low, with similar effects—exports were reduced and farmers switched to subsistence farming.

In the 1980s, though, a ray of hope appeared. All these governments eliminated or relaxed their price controls on food.

In 1981, for example, Somalia's government ended its monopoly on the purchase of maize and sorghum. As a result, production rose from 251,000 tons in 1980 to 491,000 tons by 1984. After Nigeria abolished all its government monopolies in 1986, farm exports surged. Even Ghana's government in 1983 greatly relaxed price controls on cocoa. The beneficial results were quickly evident. Even though the lead time between planting and harvesting cocoa is about five years, by 1989 more than one-third of the country's area planted with cocoa had been planted after 1984.

Price controls on food are not the only price controls that Third World governments have used to mess up their economies. Many of these governments have also imposed very repressive usury laws, thus preventing capital from flowing to its highest-valued uses. In many of these countries that have practiced what economists call "financial repression," governments have stepped in to ration credit.

The unintended consequences are twofold. First, the usury laws divert savings away from the formal financial system and drive lending underground. Second, the credit that does flow through the "above-ground" system tends to go to those who are politically favored. Both results are a drag on economic growth.

In 1983, Ramgopal Agarwala, a World Bank economist, graded thirty-one poor countries for their degree of price distortion in the 1970s. He included in his measure price controls on food and other domestic goods, usury laws, and tariffs and nontariff barriers. He found a high negative correlation between the degree of price distortion and the rate of economic growth in the 1970s. Growth rates of the ten countries with the most distorted price systems were on average two percentage points below the average for the thirty-one countries. Similarly, the ten least distorted economies had an average growth rate two percentage points above the average. Again, more evidence that price controls wreak havoc.

Avoid High Inflation. In principle, say some economists, even high inflation rates should not necessarily have a huge negative impact on economic well-being. The reason is that if inflation is high and steady, and if the country's tax system adjusts for inflation, then inflation simply amounts to a very stiff tax on holding money. People would then respond to this tax by holding less money and by changing prices more often. Using the standard economists' formula for measuring this loss, I calculate that the efficiency loss from doubling the U.S. inflation rate from 5 percent to 10 percent, for example, amounts to less than $3 billion, or only about .05 percent of U.S. GDP.

But now let's consider the real world. In that world, high inflation imposes a much larger loss. There are two crucial differences between the real world and those economists' hypothetical world.

First, the tax system is not typically indexed very well for inflation. Capital gains, for example, are computed as the difference between the price of an asset when bought and the price when sold. But inflation would drive the price higher even if the real, inflation-adjusted price did not change. The result is that the hapless seller is taxed on a phantom gain. Because the tax is paid only after the asset owner realizes the capital gain by selling the asset, asset holders have a strong incentive not to sell the asset. The efficiency loss for the economy comes about because people keep assets in their current uses rather than shifting them to higher-valued uses.

Similarly, interest paid to lenders, in a high-inflation economy, is mainly an adjustment for the depreciating value of the money in which it is paid. Yet even this inflation-adjustment-component of interest is typically taxed, giving people a strong incentive not to save.

Even if the tax system were perfectly indexed for inflation, a second element of real economies causes high inflation to have pernicious effects. That second element is inflation's variability and, therefore, unpredictability. Rarely is high inflation steady. Instead, it swings dramatically from year to year. This makes all but the shortest-run planning very difficult and thus discourages long-run investments.

Even worse than high variable inflation combined with a non-indexed tax system is lower inflation combined with price controls. West Germany after World War II illustrated this. If prices had been free to fluctuate, they would have been only about four times higher in 1948 than in 1936 because the money supply was four times more. The implied average inflation rate for those twelve years would have been only 14 percent, high by U.S. standards but trivial by Latin American standards. But prices were allowed to increase by only 31 percent, not 400 percent, turning almost half of an economy to barter. The West German case shows starkly the incredibly destructive effect that inflation combined with price controls can have.

But are not price controls what governments are supposed to do to avoid inflation? Not exactly. Price controls do not end inflation at all. Price controls hide inflation and, in hiding it, cause even more damage.

Inflation is caused when governments increase the money supply much more quickly than the growth in the economy's output. I would say that governments cause inflation by printing money. But some governments that have had high inflation have not printed it. Peru's government in the 1980s shipped it in by the boatload.

To end high inflation, governments must simply stop doing what they do to cause it. This usually requires two things. The first is currency reform. Changing the currency unit signals to people that the government intends to bring inflation down by slowing the rate of growth of the money supply. The second requirement for fighting inflation is that governments make credible commitments to not reinflate the economy. The main measure that has worked to establish credibility is to balance the government's budget. Governments typically print money, or ship it in, because they need the revenue. One way to convince people that the government is dedicated to a noninflationary path is to balance the budget without any revenue generated by inflation.

Bolivia accomplished this happy reform in 1985. When the Bolivian government adopted its New Economic Policy in August 1985, inflation was running at 60 percent a month. As well as ending usury laws, firing government employees, freezing government employee wages, repealing the laws that prevented even private-sector employers from firing employees, and cutting the marginal tax rate (the top marginal tax rate was cut from 30 percent in 1984 to 10 percent in 1990), the government announced that it would balance its budget—daily.

The finance minister kept his word, refusing to sign any checks for which there was not revenue in the government's account. Inflation fell like a rock. In the three years after 1985, the monthly inflation rate averaged 12 percent, 1 percent, and 1 percent. By early 1989, street traders were so confident in Bolivia's currency that, rather than mobbing people with American money as they had in 1985, they often refused U.S. dollars in payment.

Although Bolivia is the most dramatic example of a Latin American country whipping inflation, it is by no means the only one. The governments of Chile, Mexico, and Argentina have also made great progress. Between 1985 and 1993, Chile's inflation rate fell from 30 percent to 12 percent, Mexico's from 58 percent to 8 percent, and Argentina's from 672 percent to 7 percent. At the same time, all three countries moved from budget deficits to surplus. Interestingly, all three have done so under economic policy-makers who earned their Ph.D.s in U.S. graduate economics programs.

One little indicator of progress on inflation in Latin America is the existence of coin-operated vending machines. Until recently, there were none. The currency was losing value so rapidly that vending machines would have had to be adjusted too frequently to be profitable. But recently, because of the much more stable currencies, coin-operated vending machines have appeared.

Avoid High Marginal Tax Rates at All Income Levels. In 1979, newly elected Prime Minister Margaret Thatcher cut the United Kingdom's top tax rate on earned income from 83 percent to 60 percent and on so-called "unearned" income (income from interest and dividends) from 98 percent to 60 percent. President Ronald Reagan in 1981, along with Congress, cut marginal tax rates by 23 percent over three years and cut the top tax rate from 70 percent to 50 percent immediately. Following their example, many countries around the world cut marginal tax rates at all income levels. And these were not just minor countries. The countries that cut the top marginal tax rate by over 20 percent include the United States, Japan, the United Kingdom, Italy, South Korea, Turkey, Sweden, Brazil, Indonesia, and Australia—countries whose combined GDPs accounted for over half of world production in the early 1980s.

These tax cuts led to economic booms virtually everywhere they were tried. The most well-known economic boom, of course, was in the United States. The 1981 tax cut helped spur the longest peacetime expansion since World War II, an expansion that lasted from November 1982 to July 1990.

In 1986, Thatcher cut the top rates further, to 40 percent. Annual growth in Britain, which had averaged only 1.2 percent in the previous twelve years, shot up to 4 percent a year between 1985 and 1989.

South Korea's government cut the top rate from 70 percent to 55 percent over the years 1981 to 1984, the same years as the Reagan cut. It reduced the bottom tax rate from 8 percent to 6 percent from 1981 to 1982. Between 1981 and 1989, South Korea's economic growth averaged 9.3 percent a year, and, interestingly, the amount of inflation-adjusted taxes paid by people in the highest brackets increased substantially.

After Turkey's top rate was slashed from 75 to 50 percent, and its minimum rate was cut from 40 percent to 25 percent, its annual economic growth jumped to nearly 7 percent in the following four years and to 9 percent in 1990. Similarly, economic booms followed cuts in top tax rates in Belgium, Austria, the Netherlands, Mauritius, Egypt, Jamaica, Colombia, Chile, Bolivia, and Mexico.

Why did such cuts in marginal tax rates lead to economic booms? The reason is that the marginal tax rate is the price people pay to the government for earning income. When the price falls, people will find ways of earning more—by working harder, working smarter, working longer, and moving from the underground economy to the above-ground economy. Similarly, a reduction in the marginal tax rate raises the cost of taking deductions, causing people to take fewer deductions.

Here is how economists Reinhard B. Koester and Roger C. Kormendi put it: "Holding average tax rates constant, a 10 percentage point reduction in marginal tax rates would yield a 15.2 percent increase in per capita income for LDCs [less developed countries]."

As important as the level of the top marginal tax rate is the income threshold at which it takes effect. Raising the top marginal rate to 90 percent for only incomes above $5 million a year, for example, would have little effect on the U.S. economy other than to encourage emigration of the wealthiest people and to reduce slightly the amount of revenue collected by the government. But raising the rate to 90 percent on incomes above, for example,

$40,000 would either destroy the U.S. economy or, much more likely, make tax cheating the national pastime.

This threshold issue is crucial for developing economies. Alan Reynolds points out that very high marginal tax rates in some developing economies take effect at very low incomes. In Western Samoa, for example, the top tax rate of 50 percent in 1984 applied to all income above $4,700, which happened to be Western Samoa's per capita income. Peru and Bolivia were more extreme in 1984. There, the top marginal tax rates of 65 percent and 30 percent applied to annual incomes of $40 and $47 respectively.

In such extreme situations, cuts in tax rates will pay for themselves by generating enough new taxable activity to expand the tax base by a higher percent than the percent reduction in tax rates. The net result would be higher revenue from tax cuts. This was the key insight of the supply-siders, and it applied dramatically to such extreme cases as Peru and Bolivia.

It almost applied to the United States as well. The most careful study of Ronald Reagan's 1981 tax cuts thus far was conducted by Lawrence Lindsey, now a member of the Federal Reserve Board of Governors. Lindsey finds that those cuts cost the Treasury $114.9 billion in 1985 but gained back $81.9 billion due to the increased taxable income that they generated, for a net loss to the Treasury of $30 billion. These are impressive numbers, and no one has come forward with a cogent critique of the method that Lindsey used to generate them. Interestingly, Lindsey's numbers show that, contrary to the belief of the critics of tax cuts, Reagan's economists actually underestimated the increase in taxable income that his tax cuts would generate. Nevertheless, because the taxes did not fully pay for themselves, additional budget cuts were needed. This is true for most countries that cut marginal tax rates. To achieve economic prosperity, they should cut marginal tax rates and government spending.

What to Do

Deregulate. Peruvian economist Hernando de Soto made a name for himself by documenting the chilling effect that regulation had on Peru. De Soto noticed, as did many people, that Peru had a huge underground economy. The phrase "underground economy" implies that transactions are not very visible. But in Peru, many underground businesses are conducted out in the open.

If, for example, while in Peru you catch a bus with a lettered destination sign, chances are that the bus is part of the underground economy. Or if you buy shoes, you might buy them from one of the many small illegal manufacturers who, work out in the open. Many houses, also, are on illegally claimed property. In Peru, "underground," in short, means "illegal."

Why do so many Peruvian producers operate illegally? Because, reports de Soto, it is extremely difficult, and often impossible, to be in business legally, especially if one is not willing or able to bribe enough officials.

De Soto had some associates apply for all the permissions required to run a small garment factory in Peru. Their guideline was that they were to try to minimize the time required to get the various licenses, but not to bribe officials to do so unless refusing to pay a bribe would bring the project to a permanent halt.

They found that to start a small garment factory required complying with eleven bureaucratic procedures, took 289 days, and two bribes. The reward for such a daunting effort is that once legal, the business's owners have the privilege of paying taxes. As a result of such detailed regulation, a common saying in more than one Latin American country is "The economy grows at night—while the government is sleeping."

If people can circumvent such detailed regulation, does it really affect economic growth? Actually, yes.

The basic problem is that property rights are not efficiently protected in such a situation. When one makes a contract with someone in the underground economy who then fails to live up to the contract's terms, there is no legal recourse. As a result, long-term contracts, one of the key requirements for large long-term investments, are virtually impossible in the underground sector.

Also, because concealing a large illegal business from even occasional government monitoring is difficult, staying in the underground sector prohibits a company from exploiting economies of scale in production. It is absurd, for example, even in Latin America, for shoes to be manufactured in someone's home. And the difficulty that the government has put in the way of owning property means that squatters' rights are insecure. Therefore, those who illegally live on public property are very hesitant to build expensive dwellings.

Allow and Enforce Property Rights. Crucially important for economic growth, as Adam Smith noted in *The Wealth of Nations* and as Nobel laureate Douglass North and coauthor Robert Thomas have pointed out in the modem era, is that people are secure in their property rights. This implies an important role for government: to enforce contracts and to record and enforce property rights. It also implies a limitation on government: It must refrain from expropriating property, especially in an arbitrary fashion. If people do not feel secure in their property rights—either because government is not enforcing or is itself violating those rights—they are much less willing to invest and produce.

Gerald W. Scully, an economist at the University of Texas in Dallas, recently wrote *Constitutional Environments and Economic Growth*, a book showing the importance of enforcement of property rights and the rule of law. For 115 economies from 1960 to 1980, Scully relates growth rates of real per capita GDP to property rights. He finds that what he calls "politically open societies"—societies that bind themselves to the rule of law, to private property, and to the market allocation of resources—have growth rates of 2.7 percent, three times the rate for societies where these freedoms are much more limited.

What Doesn't Matter Much

One factor that is surprisingly unimportant for economic growth is natural resources. There is little relationship between a country's natural resource base and its degree of economic development. Two of the most resource-rich countries in the world are Russia and Brazil. Both countries, especially Russia, are in terrible economic shape. Hong Kong, on the other hand, which is nothing but a rock at the edge of the ocean—and not even a large rock—is doing quite well economically.

Nor does past economic performance guarantee future economic success. If it did, then Argentina would not have reached its sad state of a few years ago. In 1900, Argentina had the sixth highest per capita income in the world. But in 1946, Juan Peron took over the government and poisoned its politics and its economy until his death in 1974. Indeed, the effects of Peronism outlasted Peron. Peronism in economics was essentially a form of fascism. Three key elements of Peron's economic policies were strict price controls, sudden arbitrary expropriations, and class warfare. By 1990, Argentina's per capita income was fortieth in the world, slightly ahead of Malaysia and slightly behind Iran. Its per capita GNP was less than one-ninth that of the United States.

The United States can learn about growth from every other country's experience, and from what has worked and what has not worked. Indeed, that is why within economics the studies of economic growth and of economic development have merged in the last few years.

The basic lesson to be learned from the postwar evidence on countries' economic growth is that growth's major enemy is heavy government intervention—whether through tariffs, price controls, high taxes, lavish government spending, or detailed regulation. Therefore, the way to increase economic well-being is to scale back government dramatically. This does not mean that government should do nothing. It has a crucial role—to protect its citizens from foreign invasion, to protect them from each other, to maintain and enforce property rights, and to enforce contracts. But most functions that it performs beyond those few hamper not only freedom but also economic well-being.

BARBARIAN HORSES AT THE GATE[4]

Mometsu, Japan—The cool grass paddocks and tidy stables go on for mile after mile here on Japan's northern island of Hokkaido, home to this hyper-crowded country's most unlikely industry: horse breeding.

But the bucolic landscape masks a frantic economic struggle over foreign trade and Japan's national passion for horse racing. After decades of protectionism, Japan is cautiously opening its race tracks—and a good chunk of the $1 billion in annual prize money they hand out—to foreign thoroughbreds.

And the breeders at the region's 1,500 family farms, which produce about 10,000 horses a year, are panicking. They bluntly

[4]Article by Edmund L. Andrews, staff writer, from *The New York Times* 33 S 30 '95. Copyright © 1995 by The New York Times Company. Reprinted with permission.

admit their horses are no match for the faster imports from the United States, Australia, and Europe. "We just can't compete," complained Kazushi Takayame, owner of a tiny farm that breeds about six stallions and mares a year. "If foreign horses are allowed in too quickly, we will be swept out of all the top races and we won't be able to stay in business."

This might just be another tale of a once-coddled national industry's fight to survive in the global marketplace except for one thing: Japan is far and away the most horse-crazy country in the world and political loyalties are divided. Japanese placed $38 billion in bets . . . [during 1994] down from $40.8 billion in 1993, but still far more than any other country and four times the amount bet in the United States. Its $1 billion in total purse money exceeds that of any other country. When a typhoon brushed by Tokyo [during August 1995], 46,000 people still turned up at the track . . .

Japan is also the only country with a satellite television network devoted entirely to broadcasting horse races. The country has more than a dozen daily newspapers devoted to racing results.

Besides having access to hundreds of off-track betting parlors, Japanese can set up accounts over a telephone service called *WINS* and place bets by pressing buttons on the phone dial. Promoters are even experimenting with automated teller machines in convenience stores.

The upshot is that millions of people have an interest in the debate on foreign horses, and many people want to see more of them. Japan has a well-founded reputation for fighting imports of everything from rice to auto parts, but the real pressure to open up this market has not come from foreign governments as much as it has from racing promoters and horse owners within Japan.

"People say this is all because of foreign pressure, but it is really because we wanted to bring the level of Japanese horse racing up to world standards," said Norio Sakai, a spokesman for the Japan Racing Association, the agency that both regulates and promotes horse racing in Japan. "If we introduce foreign breeds, we can hold more exciting races for our fans. It doesn't make sense to keep the market closed forever while much faster horses are competing around the world."

Japanese racing fans have hardly been opposed to foreign horses either. "My feeling is that 70 to 80 percent of fans, especially young fans, are eager to have foreign horses because it will be more exciting," said Yasuhiko Amano, the horse-racing editor at *Nikkan Sports*, a newspaper in Tokyo.

Slowly but surely, Japanese horse buyers are abandoning the farms here in favor of the auction grounds of Kentucky and Ireland. As they do, the breeders here are scrambling to upgrade their stock with foreign bloodlines.

But the payoff could be a long time coming. Meantime, prices for Japanese thoroughbreds have plunged by almost half in [a few] years. Making matters worse, many Japanese breeders are getting squeezed by loans they took against their property before land prices crashed.

It would be hard to find an industry more incongruous in Japan than thoroughbred farming. The soil is high in acid and low in calcium, making it difficult to grow the mineral-rich grasses that horses thrive on. The land is exorbitantly expensive. And the horses are slow by international standards.

But the breeders have prospered ever since World War II, largely because foreign horses were flatly excluded from about 85 percent of the 3,400 national races sponsored by the Japan Racing Association.

Then, three years ago, the association announced plans to let foreign horses that had not raced in other countries compete in 55 percent of races by 1996. It also called for opening twelve of the most prestigious races to horses that had competed overseas, a move that Japanese breeders vigorously oppose.

Though the original schedule has now been stretched out to 1999, about 47 percent of the 3,400 races have been opened up—at least partly—over the last [few] years.

Breeders say the mere threat of competition has already had a big impact. Takashi Sasaki, who produces about sixteen horses a year, estimates that the top price for a stallion has dropped from more than $500,000 at the height of Japan's economic boom in 1991 to about $250,000 today. The average price for a solid mare, he figures, has declined from about $100,000 to $60,000.

Meanwhile, Japanese owners imported as many as 500 horses in 1995—the first trickle in what is expected to be an expanding flow from the United States and Europe. There are still a number of trade barriers, including a tariff on imported horses and restrictions in many races on the number of foreign-bred animals that can compete.

But buyers are clearly looking outward. "There's no animosity by the owners — it's just a simple calculation of price," said Mr. Sasaki, an earthy man who chain-smokes Lark cigarettes as he talks. "We used to set up the price by figuring our costs and a profit and presenting it to the owners. But now people are saying they would rather go to the United States to buy."

Japanese breeders, fearful of being blown out of business, are themselves shopping overseas. Toshiyuki Shimokobe, who owns one of the largest breeding operations in the region, said he paid $4.5 million in 1994 for a horse called *Afleet* and would have bought another American stallion . . . except the prices were too forbidding.

With sales of home-grown horses slumping, Mr. Shimokobe figures he has to take drastic action. "At the largest auction in Japan . . . , they tried to sell 823 horses but only 202 of them were bought," he said. "The amount paid for those horses was about $11 million, which is just a little more than what Japanese buyers paid for thirty-six horses . . . [in 1995] at the Keeneland auction in Kentucky. If those owners hadn't gone to Kentucky, they would have spent more here in Japan."

Mr. Sasaki, though he runs a much smaller operation, has also gone international. Six years ago, he bought a foal in England while it was still being carried by its mother. Now a mare called *Sweet Marjorum*, it went on to win four big races in Japan and recently gave birth to its first foal. . . . Eight of Mr. Sasaki's sixteen mares are foreign-born.

Even the Japan Racing Association, in a bid to mollify breeders, has entered the import business. It paid $10 million . . . in Kentucky for *Forty-Niner*, a ten-year-old stallion, which it gave as a gift to the breeders' cooperative here. But that only angered some of the breeders, who accused the association of overpaying and inadvertently kicking up the prices of American horses.

The United States, Australia, and New Zealand have periodically complained that their breeders were being unfairly shut out. Though the issue is too small to have arisen as a major trade dispute, it has become a pet peeve for a handful of politicians like Kentucky's Republican Senator, Mitch McConnell.

The three countries complained . . . that Japanese tracks were moving too slowly toward openness, but Japanese racing authorities said they could not move any faster than their existing plan.

The potential rewards for owners of foreign thoroughbreds are formidable. The Japan Cup, an invitation-only race that has always included big-name foreign stallions, paid about $1.5 million to the first-place winner [in 1995]—more than double the Kentucky Derby's first-place purse last year and one of the top five purses in the world. Since the Japan Cup was started in 1981, foreign horses have captured first place 9 out of 14 times.

But the real allure is in the hundreds of second-tier races. Many pay first-place winners several hundred thousand dollars, with generous purses going to second- and third-place finishers as well. Given the large number of races each year, owners of strong horses can reap millions of dollars.

That prospect has split the industry between horse owners and breeders. Owners increasingly shop the world for animals that can open the treasure chest of prize money. Breeders, who generally do not race the horses they raise, see a threat to their existence.

"We admit it, the quality of our horses is lower," said Mr. Shimokobe, the breeder. "There is no way to change that unless you get better breeding from new stallions. We're trying to do that, but it takes an enormous amount of money."

The Shimokobe farm seems a picture of prosperity. The big main building sports a manicured garden outside and expensive sedans in the driveway. Mr. Shimokobe, dressed in a fresh yellow sport shirt, talks in an almost scholarly way about the declining market for Japanese-bred horses and the need to raise millions to improve his horses' gene pool.

But while his size gives him an edge, the vast majority of small breeders face a tougher future. It is more difficult for them to raise the cash to buy top-flight foreign horses. Indeed, says Mr. Takayame, who inherited his farm from his father, many of his friends are scrambling to pay back loans. "You are lucky if you have the freedom to get out of this business," he said.

Ranchers like Mr. Takayame say they want to stay in the horse business and match world standards. But for now, they say, that requires continued protection against foreign competition, even if that seems unfair to foreign breeders.

"Japanese horses are second class; that's just the way it is," said Mr. Takayame, sipping green tea in his parlor as rain clouds rolled in from the ocean. "If we don't make enough profit, we won't have the money to buy the stronger stallions we need to surpass the Americans."

HELLO, WORLD[5]

When Kim Young Sam became president of South Korea in 1992 he announced that "globalization" would be a central theme of his administration. South Korean society would become less introverted. The economy would become more open to foreign goods and investment.

Foreign businessmen were pleased, but skeptical. Recent South Korean actions have only added to the doubts. On April 9, [1995] the finance ministry announced that, after a splurge of foreign investment by South Korean conglomerates, the government was making it harder for Koreans to invest overseas. Meanwhile, the transport ministry is thought to be reconsidering a plan to allow foreigners to bid for contracts to build a proposed high-speed railway. American trade hawks, battering at South Korea's doors, point out that foreign cars still account for only .2 percent of the South Korean market.

So is the globalization of South Korea just an empty slogan? Listen to Park Jin, the president's spokesman, and you might be more open-minded. The cosmopolitan Mr. Park, who spent several years as an academic in Britain, argues that South Korea, despite its success in building the 11th-largest trading economy in the world, has in many ways been cut off from international society. Single-minded concentration on economic growth made South Korea self-centered and inward-looking. Cold-War politics did not help: the country did not even join the United Nations until 1991.

Things are now changing. . . . South Korea is likely to get a temporary seat on the Security Council and [in 1996] . . . it will almost certainly join the OECD. Mr. Park notes proudly that a South Korean has become deputy head of the World Trade Organization.

But the economic implications of globalization are trickier. Mr. Park insists that the government wants to "encourage more

[5]Article by Michael Rogers, from *The Economist* 337:44 O 14 '95. Copyright © 1995 by The Economist Newspaper Group, Inc. Reprinted with permission. Further reproduction prohibited.

foreign participation in Korean society." But this involves something more than the usual struggles against powerful domestic lobbies. Mr. Park says it calls for a "real psychological revolution" for South Koreans, who have been brought up on a mercantilist philosophy of self-reliance.

Pinning down the extent of South Korean protectionism is difficult. Those trying to lever open the country's markets sometimes portray it as a garrison economy, from which foreign goods are all but barred. That is a caricature. South Korea actually runs a trade deficit which reflects, in large part, its industry's heavy dependence on parts from Japan. And, though consumer goods are only 11 percent of South Korea's imports, foreign brands are increasingly visible in Seoul. The computer sections in Seoul department stores carry IBM products alongside their South Korean competitors. The ice-cream parlor on the top floor of one comes courtesy of America's Baskin-Robbins.

Foreign ice-cream may be gobbled up, but other foreign goods are consumed less voraciously. In a completely free market, more foreign cars would make it on to the streets of Seoul. As ever, the Americans are leading the chorus of complaints. But at least some of their cars are allowed into South Korea; Japan's are banned.

Protectionist thinking remains deeply ingrained in South Korea. Asked to explain why South Korea's car industry succeeded, where its chemical and machine-tool industries have failed, one leading South Korean economist explains that, unfortunately, it was not practicable to ban imports of chemicals or machine tools.

But attempting to stick a protectionist label on South Korea is not as easy as it may seem. Egregious examples like the ban on Japanese cars are relatively rare. Most South Korean tariffs are pretty low. People who want to open the South Korean market must therefore poke around in the murky world of non-tariff barriers.

There is no doubt that the South Koreans have ways of discouraging imports. Until recently buyers of foreign cars often found themselves audited by the taxman. When foreign films began to gain a following, there was a rash of incidents in which snakes appeared mysteriously in cinemas showing Hollywood hits. A consignment of 140m frozen American sausages was recently held in port for months on health grounds—an incident that the Americans are now threatening to use as the basis for action under their draconian 301 trade law.

But the real frustration for would-be exporters is that the ultimate non-tariff barrier may be the national psychology of South Korea. Many South Koreans have been brought up to believe that it is unpatriotic to buy imported goods. In the 1960s civil servants found that smoking foreign cigarettes put them at risk of losing their jobs. Traces of that way of thinking linger on.

If globalization really requires a psychological change, American trade negotiators might consider a new tack. Heavy-handed American tactics in the recent car talks have set off a nationalist backlash. South Koreans who favor a more open economy are alarmed. Young Soogil, a prominent economist in Seoul, frets that his fellow countrymen are now so worked up about American pressure that they have lost sight of the fact that market opening is in their own interests.

Mr. Young has his own definition of globalization. For thirty years his countrymen have worked furiously to escape from poverty. Now they need to change their "growth psychology" and think about things that concern other rich nations, such as the arts, civil liberties, and the environment. That, he says, "would really be development." Asked if the economy can keep growing at a breakneck 8–9 percent a year, he looks out at the smog on the Seoul skyline and utters a heartfelt sigh: "I hope not."

BIBLIOGRAPHY

An asterisk (*) preceding a reference indicates that the article or part of it has been reprinted in this book.

BOOKS AND PAMPHLETS

Abbott, Frederick M. Law and policy of regional integration. M. Nijhoff. '95.

Barry, Tom. Zapata's revenge. South End. '95.

Belous, Richard S. & Lemco, Jonathan, eds. NAFTA as a model of development. State University of New York Press. '95.

Bliss, C. J. Economic theory and policy for trading blocks. Manchester University Press. '94.

Butler, David A. Does "independent" mean "free from influence?" Garland. '95.

Capie, Forrest. Tariffs and growth. Manchester University Press. '94.

Cheetham, Janet H., ed. Immigration practice and procedure under NAFTA. American Immigration Lawyers Association. '95.

Collins, Susan M. & Bosworth, Barry P., eds. The new GATT. Brookings Institution. '94.

Connolly, Michael B. & De Melo, Jaime, eds. The effects of protectionism on a small country. World Bank. '94.

Cook, Paul & Nixson, Frederick, eds. The move to the market? St. Martin's. '95.

Deardorff, Alan V. & Stern, Robert M. The Stolper-Samuelson theorem. University of Michigan. '94.

Domenica, Michael F., ed. Integrated water resources planning for the 21st century. American Society of Civil Engineers. '95.

Dryden, Steve. Trade warriors. Oxford University Press. '95.

Ebeling, Richard M. & Hornberger, Jacob G., eds. The case for free trade and open immigration. Future of Freedom Foundation. '95.

Echeverri-Carroll, Elsie L., ed. NAFTA and trade liberalization in the Americas. University of Texas. '95.

Eckes, Alfred E. Opening America's market. University of North Carolina Press. '95.

Halbach, Axel J. Regional economic development in the Middle East. Weltforum Verlag. '95.

Killgore, Mark W. & Eaton, David J. NAFTA handbook for water resource managers and engineers. American Society of Civil Engineers. '95.

Kirshner, Orin, ed. The Bretton Woods-GATT system. M.E. Sharpe. '96.

Kroll, John A. Closure in international politics. Westview. '95.

Krooth, Richard. Mexico, NAFTA, and the hardships of progress. McFarland. '95.

Leycegui, Beatriz; Robson, William B. P.; & Stein, S. Dahlia, eds. Trading punches. National Planning. '95.

Magraw, Daniel B. NAFTA and the environment. American Bar Association. '95.

McGee, Robert W. A trade policy for free societies. Quorum. '94.

Mucciaroni, Gary. Reversals of fortune. Brookings Institution. '95.

Ndlovu, Lindani B. The system of protection and industrial development in Zimbabwe. Avebury. '94.

Nevaer, Louis E. V. Strategies for business in Mexico. Quorum. '95.

Norton, Joseph J. & Bloodworth, Thomas L., eds. NAFTA and beyond. M. Nijhoff. '95.

Roberts, Russell D. The choice. Prentice Hall. '94.

Rosenberg, Jerry M. Encyclopedia of NAFTA, the new American community, and Latin-American trade. Greenwood. '95.

Runge, C. Ford; Ortalo-Magne, Francois; & Vande Kamp, Philip. Freer trade, protected environment. Council on Foreign Relations. '94.

Sazanami, Yoko; Urata, Shujiro; & Kawai, Hiroki. Measuring the costs of protection in Japan. Institute for Int. Economics. '95.

Suzumura, Kotaro. Competition, commitment, and welfare. Clarendon. '95.

Wolf, Martin. The resistible appeal of fortress Europe. American Enterprise Institution. '94.

ADDITIONAL PERIODICAL ARTICLES WITH ABSTRACTS

For those who wish to read more widely on the subjects of free trade and protectionism, this section contains abstracts of additional articles that bear on the topic. Readers who require a comprehensive list of materials are advised to consult the *Readers' Guide to Periodical Literature* and other Wilson indexes.

Crossing the line? Bud Ward. *American Journalism Review* 17:12-3 Ja/F '95

John Stossel, a correspondent for ABC's *20/20*, apparently violated an ABC policy forbidding editorial staff from advocating positions on controversial issues. Stossel's April 1994 *20/20* special "Are We Scaring Ourselves to Death?" suggested that federal environmental, health, and safety regulations are misguided, a stand that many conservative and industry groups embrace. . . . Stossel advanced his free market philosophy in speeches—some for which he was paid—before some of these groups. In one speech, Stossel advocated abolishing the Food and Drug Administration. ABC director of news media relations Teri Everett says that Stossel's call for shutting down the FDA and other federal agencies did not violate any network policy because it was not a subject of current controversy. Another ABC policy, which was to go into effect January 1, [1995] has placed a ban on honoraria for speaking to for-profit businesses and trade associations.

Costs, competition drive labor issues. James Ott. *Aviation Week & Space Technology* 143:46–8 N 20 '95

Relations between airlines and labor are undergoing considerable changes as free trade spreads around the world and protectionism fights its final battles. Rigorous competition is pressuring management to cut costs as never before. For labor, concessions and pay cuts have characterized much of the early part of this decade, and job security has emerged as its chief concern. More recently, however, unions say that employees have conceded more than their share to keep airlines, which are now turning profits, afloat. Union leaders are now interested in wage and benefit improvements.

Arguing for free trade. Paul Johnson. *Commentary* 100:50–1 Ag '95

All sensible people want free trade to expand in the 21st century, and most people believe that it will. The realization of this optimistic scenario will not be automatic, however. If things are left to fate, mercantilists within the European Union will lead the way toward an anti-free-trade approach culminating in the division of the world into three implacably hostile trading blocks. To prevent such an outcome, the U.S. should encourage and cooperate with Britain in its efforts to resist mercantilism and create a European free-trade area.

Current status of U.S. trade. *Congressional Digest* 73:261–3+ N '94

Part of an issue on the General Agreement on Tariffs and Trade (GATT). The end of the Cold War means a new era for trade between the United States and the rest of the world. U.S. domestic and economic priorities are no longer subordinate to foreign policy priorities—instead, these goals now work in tandem. In addition, the rise of the global economy requires the U.S. to remain engaged in the world. The article reviews the trade status of the U.S. in 1993 and discusses the nation's export growth, imports, service exports and rising trade deficit and the impact of trade on the U.S. economy.

The propaganda way. Kishore Mahbubani. *Foreign Affairs* 74:193-6 My/Je '95

Rather than the glue that holds Asian societies together, Asian values may be an illusion concealing the strong hold of petty despots. Various commentators have asserted that unique Asian values are responsible for the high rates of economic growth in East Asia. This commentary, however, reflects an important trait arising out of Asian customs. Evaluations of government that are not characterized by unconditional praise for the Asian political status quo provoke a strong response from the powers that be. In this manner, Asian authoritarian regimes are attempting to impose cultural protectionism to isolate their communities from infectious liberalizing Western influences. Just as trade protection stagnates economic growth, so cultural protection inhibits cultural progress. Cultural protectionism also slows the formation of an information-based economy and handicaps economic growth.

Consolidating capitalism. Jeffrey D. Sachs. *Foreign Policy* 98:50-64 Spr '95

. . . A global capitalist economy seems possible for the first time. Countries with a combined population of roughly 3.5 billion have undergone radical economic reforms to incorporate the institutions of the capitalist system. These reforms are characterized by open international trade, currency convertibility, private ownership as the catalyst for economic growth, corporate ownership of large enterprises, openness to foreign investment, and membership in key international economic institutions. Weak U.S. leadership and fractious relations between industrial democracies, however, are already endangering the opportunity to create a prosperous and law-bound international system. The writer discusses the development of the capitalist world over the past 150 years; the need to consolidate market reforms in Russia, China, and Africa and resist protectionism on the part of developed countries; and the importance of an international rule of law in holding the system together.

Taking Pat Buchanan seriously. John B. Judis. *Gentlemen's Quarterly* 65:230-7+ D'95

Republican Pat Buchanan is once again campaigning to run for president. Buchanan has modified his most divisive rhetoric from his 1992 campaign, and his "core issues" are trade, jobs, wages, and immigration. He is the only presidential candidate to propose constitutional amendments to ban abortion and pornography, permit school prayer, and stop illegal aliens getting benefits and becoming citizens. Although he was once are solute free trader and a Cold War interventionist, Buchanan is now a protectionist and an isolationist, pledging to remove the United Nations from the United States. Buchanan sometimes appears to be a populist who articulates the economic concerns of working-class Americans, but he can also be seen as a xenophobe who summons up the dark intolerance and fanaticism of the old right.

The gall of Goldsmith. Joseph Nocera. *Gentlemen's Quarterly* 65:73-4+ Je '95

Sir James Goldsmith, a high-profile corporate raider during the 1980s, is now the author of a book that deplores the lean and mean corporate atmosphere that he and his ilk helped create. *The Trap* is suspicious of multinational corporations and scientific progress, opposed to agribusiness and nuclear energy, full of dire warnings about the welfare state yet stuffed with proposals that would make the welfare state even bigger, and all the while imbued with the belief that smaller is always better. Goldsmith also now believes that the General Agreement on Tariffs and Trade will bring about the destruction of the world as we know it. What hasn't changed is that Goldsmith remains unburdened by self-doubt. He is among the many rich people who have succumbed to the delusion that wealth bestows wisdom. Before Goldsmith has earned the right to be listened to, he has a lot to atone for.

Divide and multiply in 1996. Scott Tucker. *The Humanist* 55:40-2 S/O '95

The author outlines some problems with President Clinton and the Democratic party in such areas as constitutional and civil rights, welfare and health care, and foreign policy and human rights.

Stakeholders versus stockholders: the populist challenge to "free trade." Steven Hill. *The Humanist* 55:17-21 Mr/Ap '95

A populist challenge is growing in the United States against "free trade." With occasional assistance from state and local governments, abandoned communities are devising new strategies for fighting back against corporate greed, disinvestment, and autocracy. Two noteworthy cases of community resistance were the anti-takeover corporate law passed in Pennsylvania in 1990 and a Michigan judge's 1993 order blocking General Motors' plans to relocate its Ypsilanti assembly plant to Arlington, TX. At issue in both cases were the rights of the stakeholders—the workers and local citizens—versus the rights of private corporations.

Getting down to the business of business. Diane Francis. *Maclean's* 108:9 S 4 '95

The electoral victories of the Reform party federally and the Tories in Alberta, Manitoba, and Ontario signal that Canadians are beginning to realize that the business of Canada must be business. The ascension of free trade is irreversible and requires huge reforms because the only players who will profit will be those whose governments are efficient and business-oriented and whose policies encourage free enterprise. Nations can no longer afford to indulge in nationalism and socialism, to run deficits and rack up huge debts, to pay many of the costs associated with the welfare state, to have environmental restrictions greater than those imposed by competing nations, or to have one-sided labor laws that favor unions and entrenched unionization.

Shoot the Keynesians. Deirdre McMurdy. *Maclean's* 108:36 Mr 20 '95

Part of a cover story on international finance. Some economists believe that global currency market speculation and the volatility that it engenders are evil and must be exorcized. These economists contend that wild, recurring swings in currency rates undermine carefully structured government policies and erode national sovereignty. According to this pious lot, the traders who whip billions of dollars around the world each day in a search for profit are really agents of international chaos. In support of such thinking, the rabid Keynesian and Nobel laureate American economist James Tobin has even suggested that market speculators should be deterred from their dastardly agenda with a tax of one percent on every currency trade. Such thinking reflects an urge to tamper with a classically perfect, well-balanced free market. Unfettered foreign exchange markets are valuable because they provide enormous liquidity and sniff out flaws in the global financial eco-system.

Six smart ways to cash in on free trade and GATT's fat cats. Michael Sivy. *Money* 24:71 Ja '95

Nearly every large U.S. company with sizable exports or global operations stands to benefit from the General Agreement on Tariffs and Trade's reduced tariffs, enhanced international copyright protections, and generally freer trade. This should translate into gains for investors in cost-efficient companies with access to global markets. Six companies that should reap major benefits from GATT—Merck, J. P. Morgan, General Electric, Caterpillar, United Technologies, and Boeing—are discussed.

The globetrotting sneaker. Cynthia Enloe. *Ms.* 5:10–5 Mr/Ap '95

Many Western sneaker manufacturers have established manufacturing plants in Asian countries where wages are low and government policies restrict labor organizing. The employees, mostly women, often work long hours in dangerous and humiliating conditions. Those who demand better treatment may risk dismissal, violent reprisals, and sexual assault, sometimes at the hands of government forces. When women succeed in forcing improvements in pay and working conditions, as happened in South Korea, the manufacturers or their Asian subcontractors move to other countries where labor is cheaper. Trade pacts such as the North American Free Trade Agreement and the General Agreement on Tariffs and Trade contribute to the problem because they contain few or no provisions requiring fair labor practices, healthy work environments, or respect for the right to organize.

Beyond too far. David Corn. *The Nation* 260:477–8 Ap 10 '95

The Clinton administration has had some success attempting to define it-self in response to Newt Gingrich and the Republicans, but the President has so far been unwilling to name and blame the corporate and transna-tional bullies who will benefit from the *Contract With America*. A promising model for the Democrats' next step has been offered by House minority leader Richard Gephardt, who charges that the Republicans are trying "to force us into a global economic steeplechase with no rules, no order and no standards." Advised by economist Barry Bluestone, Gephardt wants to fight economic globalization and the resulting drop in U.S. living standards through trade policies that incorporate higher labor, safety, and environmental standards abroad. He also supports more workplace democracy at home, as well as arrangements that let corporate employees share the profits from enhanced productivity.

NAFTA math. Eyal Press and Rose George. *The Nation* 260:4-5 Ja 2 '95

At the Miami Summit of the Americas, leaders pledged to create a hemi-sphere wide free-trade accord within the next decade—an agreement similar to NAFTA, only with scant mention of the side agreements on la-bor and the environment that President Clinton added as sweeteners to the original trade deal. These agreements were essentially meaningless anyway, as events in Mexico over the past year have shown. Meanwhile, despite the talk in Miami about the 100,000 new jobs that NAFTA sup-posedly created in the U.S. in its first year, a recent Congressional analysis shows that the agreement has actually cost the U.S. a net 10,000 jobs when positions related to both exports and imports are taken into ac-count.

Tex Mex. Richard Conniff. *National Geographic* 189:44-69 F '96

The border along the Rio Grande, which separates Mexico and theUnit-ed States, both divides and unites two fast-changing worlds. Since the signing of the North American Free Trade Agreement in November 1993, the Rio Grande border has become the center of the biggest free-trade deal in history. While it is not clear how liberalization of trade will ultimately change the border, some are concerned that the benefits of the agreement will ultimately bypass the border area for distant cities such as San Antonio and Monterrey. In any case, whether or not either side approves, the Mexicanization of America by immigrants and the Ameri-canization of Mexico by commercial competition and mass culture can be clearly observed in the area.

Gentleman callers. *National Review* 47:12+ O 23 '95

As outsiders, Colin Powell and Ross Perot are changing the political de-bate. If Powell runs as a Republican, he will force the other candidates to be more explicitly and intelligently conservative. Bob Dole will be forced to show an understanding of the issues, a mastery of the relevant arguments, and a passionate delivery, while Phil Gramm, Pat Buchanan, and Steve Forbes must do more than trump Dole by saying that they are more conservative. The GOP must move on term limits, campaign finance reform, protectionism, and immigration controls to return the Perot voter to the right. Both Powell and Perot supporters fantasize about national discussion unencumbered by ideology, but ideas and ideals provide the only guidance through the welter of events.

Keep America first. *National Review* 47:12+ Jl 31 '95

Republicans need to show more interest in foreign policy. Although the party remains committed to global leadership, a strong defense, and free trade, foreign policy issues only warrant its attention, as NAFTA and GATT did, when they involve domestic politics. Moreover, Republican leaders have criticized aspects of President Clinton's multilateral approach to foreign policy without offering a coherent alternative. Thus, the party's foreign policy approach is at risk of becoming operationally isolationist. Republican policy should instead be focusing on maintaining America's position as the world's sole super power.

From "dependencia" to shared prosperity. Fernando Henrique Cardoso. *New Perspectives Quarterly* 12:42–3 Wint '95

Part of a special issue on globalization. Latin American social scientists and political leaders, who once regarded the international economic system as the cause of underdevelopment and dependency in their region, now believe that the solution of their problems will require participation in that system. At the Summit of the Americas, held in Miami in December [1995], participants discussed the creation of a Hemispheric Free Trade Zone, the implementation of the General Agreement on Tariffs and Trade, the need for unobstructed access to advanced technology in conjunction with freer flows of trade and investment, and the realization that sustainable economic growth requires social justice and respect for the balance of nature. The ideologies of the past have given way to pragmatic tasks that require cooperation.

Global free trade: recipe for a lumpen planet. Sir James Goldsmith. *New Perspectives Quarterly* 12:39–41 Wint '95

Part of a special issue on globalization. If implemented, the General Agreement on Tariffs and Trade (GATT) will impoverish and destabilize the industrialized world and ravage the Third World. The developed world will face new competition from populous developing countries where unemployment is high and wages are low. Manufacturing companies will transfer production to low-cost areas, and those that do not will perish. High-tech industries will survive in the developed world, but they employ few people. In the Third World, the introduction of efficient agricultural practices will drive millions of rural people into urban slums. Instead of embracing global free trade, neighboring countries with similar economies and wage structures should form regional trade areas.

Bland ambition. Matthew Cooper. *The New Republic* 213:22+ S 18-25 '95

Republican Senator Richard Lugar of Indiana is not likely to be elected president, but he could assume the mantle of the thinking man's candidate for 1996. A self-styled foreign policy expert, Lugar backs NAFTA and offers an intellectually honest stance on Bosnia. Despite his pro-Reagan voting record, he won praise from liberal editorialists during the 1980s for his positions on South Africa and the Philippines. With a pedigree on racial issues from his stint as mayor of Indianapolis, he also has the potential to cool hot-button issues like immigration and affirmative action. He is hampered, however, by a dull personal style and a tendency toward sanctimonious preening on family values. In addition, his enthusiasm for replacing the income tax with a national sales tax puts him in the company of people who are less than moderate.

Run, Colin, run! *The New Republic* 213:9 N 20 '95

Colin Powell should run for president, even though he is not obviously preferable over the other candidates in the field. Powell is a man of many deficiencies as well as virtues. Counting against him as a candidate are his preternatural caution, his lack of a distinctive politics, his foreign policy timidity, his apologism for the military establishment, and his lack of domestic policy experience. Yet Powell, who is sane, competent, charismatic, and decent, should submit himself as a candidate if only because the far right of the GOP is desperate to keep him out of the race. The far right probably knows that its hold on the average GOP voter is tenuous; it needs to keep moderates like Powell out of the primaries and out of the party in order to win. If Powell emerged as the Republican candidate, or even if he broadened the base and tone of the Republican race, he could seriously weaken the religious right's hold on the country's dominant party.

Mexico's wake-up call. Marc Levinson. *Newsweek* 125:52-3 Ja 9 '95

Mexico's currency crash is having dire repercussions. The peso has approached near collapse, accompanied by soaring interest rates and a crashing Mexican stock market. The crisis may bring further unrest to a country that has experienced a guerrilla's uprising and two political assassinations in the past twelve months. It can also be expected to end the U.S. export boom that followed the controversial North American Free Trade Agreement. The writer discusses the challenges faced by President Ernesto Zedillo, who took office on Dec. 1, [1994] and describes the impact of the crash on foreign investors, Mexicans, Mexican companies, U.S. exporters, and Latin America.

The contemplative bomb-thrower. Joe Klein. *Newsweek* 125:37 Ja 30 '95

House Minority Whip David Bonior of Michigan has recently been road-testing incendiary populist rhetoric against the new Republican majority in Congress. Bonior adheres to two some what contradictory and clearly waning political movements: economic populism and Roman Catholic liberation theology. Among the targets of his attacks have been corporate greed and free trade with Mexico. Bonior's reputation for extreme decency and hard work has won him support, but the Republicans' message of cultural outrage against wasteful government and the immoral poor hits closer to home for many blue-collar suburbanites.

Cheap speech. Jeff Rosen. *The New Yorker* 71:75–80 Ag 7 '95

As several new books about the First Amendment suggest, the proliferation of new media outlets such as the Internet poses practical obstacles to any centralized proposals to regulate speech. Indeed, the new media technologies may dramatically fulfill Justice Holmes's metaphor of a perfectly deregulated "free trade in ideas." This ideal vision of the First Amendment may not be wholly palatable to everyone, however. Discussed are Nadine Strossen's "Defending Pornography: Free Speech, Sex, and the Fight for Women's Rights," Robert Post's "Constitutional Domains: Democracy, Community, and Management," Kent Greenawalt's "Fighting Words: Individuals, Communities, and Liberties of Speech," Patrick Garry's "Scrambling for Protection: The New Media and the First Amendment," and Newton Minow and Craig La May's "Abandoned in the Wasteland: Children, Television, and the First Amendment."

Who killed the middle class? John Cassidy. *The New Yorker* 71:113–4+ O 16 '95

Part of a special home issue. Recent wage and income trends point to the irrevocable conclusion that America, in economic terms, is no longer a middle-class country. While productivity, profits, and stock prices have soared in recent years, wages have not kept pace. Instead, living standards for the majority of Americans have fallen or stagnated, while a small minority at the top have enjoyed a bonanza. This rise in economic inequality has had nothing to do with taxation. Most economists blame some combination of trade, technology, immigration, and the decline of labor unions for the increasingly difficult plight of ordinary workers, but no one has satisfactorily explained the explosion of incomes at the top, especially among highly educated workers and big executives. Meanwhile, politicians refuse to face the fact that the free market will no longer produce rising prosperity for all.

America's role in Russia. *New York Times* A16 Ja 29 '96

The U.S. should pressure Russian President Boris Yeltsin to continue his reform efforts as parliamentary elections approach.Yeltsin's recent actions have eroded his earlier reform policies in attempts to salvage his political clout. The U.S. cannot support a Yeltsin rival since Yeltsin is still the elected President of Russia.

The foreign policy campaign. *New York Times* A32 F 16 '96

With his distinguished war record and Senate leadership on international affairs, Senator Bob Dole can set the standard for a more considered discussion of foreign policy during the presidential campaign. Dole has already played the foreign policy card in New Hampshire, which was not a bad strategy in the tight primary there. Americans prefer to be comfortable with prospective Presidents as Commander in Chief, and Dole enjoys a clear advantage over his rivals on that score.

Trucks at the border. *New York Times* A20 D 20 '95

The North American Free Trade Agreement permits freer movement of U.S. and Mexican trucks on both sides of the border, promising to dramatically increase commerce. Fears of accidents involving Mexican trucks in the North, however, along with Mexico's concerns over U.S. competition, have prompted both countries to postpone a general border opening . . . .

Winning by losing on trade. *New York Times* 14 Ja 21 '96

. . . The World Trade Organization ruled that a provision in the U.S. Clean Air Act violated free trade rules and required foreign oil producers to meet higher pollution standards than their American counterparts. This ruling was logical and fair. It also establishes the W.T.O. as a strong body willing and able to enforce rules of fair grade.

Last tango for socialism. Thomas W. Hazlett. *Reason* 26:66 Mr '95

Now that populists in the U.S. are condemning "cheap foreign labor" while the world's poor are rejecting statism in favor of the free market, socialism has revealed itself to be both intellectually and morally bankrupt. In the past, anti-market apologists could at least claim to hold the moral high ground as defenders of the poor. . . . however, capitalists like Brazil's Fernando Henrique Cardoso are being elected by poor third-world voters seeking relief from inflation, while anti-free-trade forces in the U.S. are defending comparatively rich American workers against the rising aspirations of poorer people in the rest of the world.

No deals. Brian Doherty. *Reason* 26:6–7 F '95

Congress should act unilaterally to end restrictive trade laws. Multilateral agreements such as NAFTA and GATT are not the best way to achieve free trade. Such pacts tend to be larded with complications, half-measures, and escape clauses. Moreover, they create the potential for exporting onerous regulations. Congress should act by itself to abolish anti-dumping laws, tariffs, quotas on imports, the Jones Act, and other laws that restrict or make it expensive to buy or sell goods across the U.S. border. Doing so would be great for consumers and for producers who depend on imports to get material they need for their production processes.

Northern exposures. Margot Hornblower. *Time* 145:40+ Mr 6 '95

Mexicans see their past and present in terms of a continuing tug-of-war with the U.S. Mexican students are taught a litany of humiliations that the country has suffered at the hands of its northern neighbor: The 1848 Treaty of Guadalupe Hidalgo, which forced the sale of Mexico's northern half; American invasions in 1914 and 1916; the expulsion of as many as one million Mexican immigrants from the U.S. during the 1950s Operation Wetback; and now California's Proposition 187, aimed at denying education and health services to undocumented immigrants. Nevertheless, perceptions of the U.S. are growing more sophisticated with the rapid rise of immigration to the U.S. and the explosion of commerce since the implementation of the North American Free Trade Agreement [1994].

Vietnam: back in business. Frank Gibney. *Time* 145:36–9+ Ap 24 '95

Part of a cover story on the Vietnam war. Twenty years after the war's end, Vietnam's economy and spirits are thriving. Thanks to changes in economic policy initiated over the past decade, Vietnamese can now launch their own businesses and enter into agreements with foreign investors. The lifting of the U.S. trade embargo in 1994 has also contributed to Vietnam's economic growth, which is continuing at a rate of 7 to 8 percent a year. The new prosperity of the cities has yet to reach the countryside, however, and the end of free education and health care has made life worse for many rural families. Many peasants are pouring into the cities looking for work, and prostitution has reappeared. Still, the most common complaint is that economic reform is not moving fast enough.

U.S. on dangerous protectionist path. *USA Today* 122:4–5 Ap '94

According to Stanford University economist Anne Krueger, the current U.S. trade policy is a recipe for economic and possibly political trouble. Krueger believes that although the U.S. ostensibly gave support to global free trade during the talks on the General Agreement on Tariffs and Trade, it has undermined that apparent commitment through a series of bilateral or regional trade agreements that create special relationships between the U.S. and individual nations, including Chile, Canada, and Mexico. Other nations that have endorsed free trade under U.S. prodding are recognizing the growing gap between American words and actions, she observes. Still, Krueger predicts, the U.S. will change its position when protectionism starts to erode the country's living standards.

A new tapestry of protectionism. Susan Dentzer. *U.S. News & World Report* 117:83 D5 '94

The GATT treaty, which is supposed to free up global trade, contains protection for the textile and clothing manufacturers of America and other wealthy nations. For decades, the rich nations have imposed intricate quotas and high tariffs on textiles and clothing imported from poorer nations. American tariffs on apparel average between 20 and 30 percent, while the average U.S. tariff on other goods is now 2 percent. This protection boosts the price that Americans pay for imported clothing and textiles by an estimated $9 billion per year. The new trade pact commits countries to dismantle quotas and convert them to tariffs, and then to negotiate these tariffs downward. The countries that have signed GATT have already put off the dismantling of most quotas until 2004, however, and some analysts are concerned that U.S. apparel manufacturers will lobby to push the deadline back even further.

France's man of many monuments. Fred Coleman. *U.S. News & World Report* 120:17 Ja 22 '96

Francois Mitterrand died recently at the age of 79. His long political career was built on unexpected shifts from right- to left-wing politics. During his tenure, he ended the death penalty, and his foreign policy continued France's Gaullist legacy as a fiercely independent nuclear power ultimately aligned with the United States. His architectural monuments, which include the I. M. Pei pyramid at the Louvre, the new National Library, and the science city at La Villette, changed the face of Paris. His greatest monument, however, was a united Europe, for which he worked closely with Germany's Helmut Kohl, helping to turn Western Europe into the world's largest single market and a fifteen-nation, 300 million-person entity that is still growing and moving toward greater political unity.

Hell no, they shouldn't go. Michael Barone and Jim Impoco. *U.S. News & World Report* 119:50-1 D 11 '95

President Clinton's decision to send U.S. peace keepers to Bosnia is a target of opportunity for Republican presidential candidate Pat Buchanan's blend of economic populism and Christian right social policy. Buchanan's nationalism, which features attacks on such "New World Order" institutions as the "corrupt" United Nations and the World Trade Organization and such pacts as the North American Free Trade Agreement, has been given a human face by the Bosnian intervention. Buchanan calls Clinton's plan "an act of folly" and states that Bosnia, which is not covered by NATO, is not a vital interest of the United States. Buchanan, who was an ardent supporter of the Vietnam War and a staunch advocate of free trade, has sharply shifted his views. He argues that the end of the cold war signifies that the United States has discharged its responsibilities to the world and should now look after America first.

North American Free Trade Agreement. Carlos Salinas de Gortari. *Vital Speeches of the Day* 59:742-4 O 1 '93

In a May 27, 1993, address delivered at the 75th anniversary of the Foreign Policy Association in New York City, the president of Mexico discusses his country's changing economy and the importance of the North American Free Trade Agreement (NAFTA): Over the past five years, Mexico has implemented far-reaching changes in its economic structure. After a renegotiation of Mexico's foreign debt was completed, the economy was opened up to competition, the majority of economic sectors were deregulated, non-strategic state companies were privatized, and investment and exports were promoted. As a result, Mexico is growing faster than the population growth rate, inflation has been reduced from nearly 200 percent to a rate that has reached 10 percent and is still falling, and the deficit has disappeared for a second year. The recently finalized NAFTA promises to bring further benefits to Mexico, as well as to the United States and Canada.

He's no Bill Clinton. Daniel Franklin. *The Washington Monthly* 27:10–15 My '95

Harry Truman is remembered by history as a model president, but the truth is that Bill Clinton's first two years in office have put Truman's to shame. Clinton has accomplished far more for the American people than Truman had by April 1947, guiding the economy more successfully and passing more laws with real impact. Yet while Truman is revered, Clinton has been written off as an indecisive lame duck. Clinton could still pull off the kind of comeback in 1996 that Truman did in 1948, and if he maintains his current pace, the country could see a very successful presidency. The article compares Truman and Clinton's handling of the economy; discusses Clinton's commitment to politically risky economic programs like NAFTA, his education policy, and his efforts to reduce crime; compares Truman and Clinton's records on military and foreign policy issues; and discusses the successes of Clinton's foreign policy.